How to Garden When You Rent

DK

How to Garden When You Rent

MATTHEW POTTAGE

Contents

Introduction

As both a renter and a gardener,
I want to show you just how much
you can achieve in an outdoor
space that isn't yours. With
plenty of containers and even
more imagination, any tenant
has the potential to turn their
garden into a space that feels like
theirs and where they will enjoy
spending time.

A leafy space
Despite the limited size of my
space, I've managed to create a
quiet corner to sit with a cup of
coffee or glass of wine.

My rental garden

When we moved into our current rental home in west London, I was a little disappointed that the front yard was paved over, and most of the back garden, too. The landlord gave us a vivid description of how unkempt the previous two sets of tenants had allowed the front yard to become, forcing them to pave it over, so my planned plea of removing the paving stones was not even worth airing. I told myself that perhaps there was not much point in doing anything with it—we did not plan on renting the home for long and, after all, it was not ours anyway.

The backyard was not such a sterile affair, boasting a rotting fence that was bending under the weight of a neighbor's out-of-control mile-a-minute vine, some rampant bamboo sandwiched between fences (which continues to invade about four yards), and a picnic table that was slowly composting itself from the legs up. A towering *Fatsia japonica* was a welcome surprise, though.

It wasn't long before I felt the need to improve matters. Even though I had only a handful of potted plants, and a discarded table and chairs from the restaurant at work, I quickly

For a little while, I told myself that there was not much point in doing anything with the yard—after all, we didn't own the space. Thankfully, this thought didn't last long.

The view from inside
I knew I wanted to see plants from all the doors and windows in my home.

Using shade
The side yard is a very narrow and shady space, which is great for growing foliage plants and ferns.

figured out that if we did nothing with the space, we would be the ones who lost out. Nobody else was staring at our yard except us!

Making a start

After initially finding London a rather impersonal place where it was hard to meet other people, we soon became friends with our neighbors, simply through me being in the front yard as I started to do some container gardening there. On a street with mostly paved front yards, I was a novelty with my exotic palm choices. I was fascinated by how often passers-by stopped to ask about them and comment on how they looked. Without the plants, I would have had

no reason to be in the front yard—other than to visit the trash cans, which is hardly a conversation starter!

Transformations

Life does not always work out as planned and some eight years later, for one reason or another, we still find ourselves renting the same home. However, we now have a wonderful collection of potted plants, two self-contained water features, and a micro-pond, all of which can move with us when the time comes.

If I had stubbornly done nothing with the space, simply because it wasn't ours, I would have lost so much enjoyment and well-being from time spent gardening, and perhaps we

Some eight years after moving in, for one reason or another, we still find ourselves renting the same home. However, we now have a wonderful collection of potted plants, two self-contained water features, and a micro-pond, all of which can move with us when the time comes.

wouldn't have got to know our neighbors, who have stayed friends ever since. Also, thanks to our collection of bird feeders, we appear to have become a mecca for the local sparrow population, all of whom are a pleasure to watch from the window.

Reasons to begin

It's easy to find reasons to feel discouraged or disinterested in gardening as a renter. Maybe the garden is too small, too shady, untidy, unloved, underwhelming. Maybe it's not a garden at all; maybe all you have is a yard, a balcony, a fire escape, a windowsill. Maybe you're too busy to take care of a garden. Maybe you're planning to move in the next few months, and the idea of planting some seeds feels pointless when you may not get to see them bloom. So, with all of those maybes, why bother gardening as a renter at all? Why not wait until you own a garden of your own?

- **It's all good practice.** Use gardening in a rented space as an opportunity to sharpen your teeth, practicing for the day you may get a larger garden, or own one. Many gardening principles are the same on a small scale as a large scale, and there is no such thing as a waste of effort in a garden. Even if plants die—and believe me they do in my garden, too—it's all learning and experience. The worst

Grouping plants
A simple tabletop display of
Sempervivum 'Lilac Time'
offers an interesting
color combination.

Growing tender plants

My sheltered garden is home to
many plants that people often
grow as houseplants, helped by
the warm London microclimate.

Even if your space is tiny, if everyone made an effort to add a little greenery
to their garden or outdoor spaces, suddenly a bee has a nectar source,
or a bird has somewhere to nest.

thing you can do is do nothing, for fear of getting it wrong. Nobody is born pricking out lettuce seedlings, and so much is learned from trying new things!

- **It's good for the environment.** Ever more importantly, gardening goes hand in hand with helping your local environment, which in turn, helps the climate, and the planet. Even if your space is tiny, if everyone made an effort to add a little greenery to their garden or outdoor spaces, suddenly a bee has a nectar source, or a bird has somewhere to nest. Planting can stop rainwater rushing down a drain, and a tree can help reduce the temperature around it, while absorbing carbon. These are things we all need to be acting on.
- **It's a great mental health boost.** Not only is gardening good for your physical health, it can offer a huge boost to your mental well-being, too. Spending time among plants—away from screens, notifications, and emails—helps bring a sense of calm, and there is something wholesome about nurturing and growing plants. Some of those plants might stay

with you for decades and become familiar faces in the garden, growing in sentimental value, too.

Connecting with your home

Living in rented accommodation is no longer an unusual scenario—in fact rather the opposite. Perhaps for some it's a temporary situation, while for others it might be a desirable, longer-term plan, free from being tied to a mortgage and the costs of maintaining the fabric of a building. So why not actively enjoy the outdoor space during that time? Settling into a garden can really make a house feel like a home, and help you develop an emotional connection with the space. I hope anyone looking through this book will be encouraged and empowered to start a little gardening magic in their rented outdoor space, no matter how small the garden or how inexperienced the tenant.

So, do not be perturbed by your rental situation and remember that gardening is not just about making a place look wonderful. It's also a gym without the membership fees, great for your mental health without you really knowing it, and a wider helping hand to the planet.

The realities of renting

Gardening in a rented space may not come with quite the same freedom as if you owned the place yourself, but that doesn't mean you have to limit your creativity or ambition. With the right approach—and by engaging with your landlord, roommates, and neighbors—you'll get a huge amount of pleasure and sense of well-being from your work.

Gardening as a renter

A common belief is that a rental garden can never be as beautiful as one that you own. In fact, any space has the potential to look beautiful, and impressive results can be achieved in a surprisingly short time.

Rental gardens come in all shapes and sizes, from balconies and windowsills to larger spaces with a lawn and borders. Any outdoor space offers an opportunity to learn new skills, find out what plants you like to grow, and develop your style and tastes.

Taking opportunities

Many rental spaces, especially in cities, have only a small amount of outdoor space, with little or no access to open soil—but this can be an advantage in disguise. New gardeners may find large spaces overwhelming, especially if time and budget are not readily available, whereas it's possible to achieve striking results with fewer plants on a smaller scale. If your new outdoor space is small or awkwardly shaped, use this as an opportunity to get creative with your planting and design choices, and break away from traditional ideas of what the space is "supposed" to look like. You'll find plenty of ideas to help you in the following chapters.

If you're fortunate enough to have moved into a place with plenty of outdoor space, a number of the following projects will give you scope to experiment and, depending on how long you plan to stay, to make small or large changes.

Temporary enjoyment

Perhaps one of the main differences between renting and owning is knowing that your time caring for the space will be relatively short. For some, that might be a few years; for others, a matter of months. In this book, you'll find gardening ideas and projects for a range of spaces and situations. Chapters are based around different tenancy lengths. These chapters are only a guide, however—many of the ideas will suit longer or shorter tenancies, too.

A portable garden

As a rental gardener, you may find yourself asking, "What can I take with me when I move? What am I happy to leave behind?" The obvious solution is to make the most of containers (see pp.58–63). A vast amount of gardening can be achieved in pots, including homegrown crops (see pp.106–117), trees (see pp.130–139), and even water features (see pp.140–49).

If you're lucky enough to have access to open soil, make the most of it, either with short-lived bedding plants (see pp.42–51) or longer-lasting perennials (see pp.120–129). When the time comes for you to move, you may be able to dig up some perennials and shrubs and put them into pots to take with you.

But, while it's worth thinking about what you can take when you leave, consider also what you can leave behind for the next tenants. Just as you might have appreciated inheriting a little greenery when you moved in, or enjoyed the surprise of seeing bulbs emerge from borders in spring (see pp.96–99), the new tenants may well appreciate the results of your efforts, too.

Perhaps one of the main differences between renting and owning is knowing that your time spent caring for the space is going to be relatively short. For some, that might be a few years; for others, a matter of months.

Plants and more
A key part of your space will be the plants, but adding lighting and furniture will also contribute to making it feel like your own.

Keeping your landlord happy

A tenant that actively wants to care for their garden or outdoor space is surely good news for any landlord. Even so, be sure to keep them in the loop or ask for permission for significant changes.

Careful planning
Here, the perennials and trees have been carefully selected for their impact, and the outdoor furniture complements the planting.

Start a conversation

When it comes to garden design, many landlords will have different priorities from their tenants. Some may be keen to keep their properties—including outdoor spaces—looking neutral, so they can appeal to a wide range of tenants. Others may fear damage caused by their tenants' changes, or worry that new plants will grow untidy and unsightly over time.

Arrange a conversation with your landlord to outline your plans and ask about their preferences, and find out if there are features they do not want to be changed. Share images of plants or drawings so that they can picture your ideas, and emphasize that you're intent on caring for the space and making it look more beautiful. Reassure them that you're creating something that can please everybody: you, your landlord, and possible future tenants.

Don't be afraid to ask them to chip in, either—especially when the costs are maintenance-related. As part of my plans for improving my rented garden, my landlord agreed to repair a broken fence and paint an external wall.

Work in progress

Landlords do not want to be left with unfinished construction after you've moved out, or plants that become invasive. Do your homework and only improve what is there, with minimum hassle or input from them. If your landlord does agree to major changes, don't start any project you can't complete before you leave—you'll just create a headache for the next tenant (and possibly make it difficult to reclaim all of your deposit).

As you progress, send your landlord photos every now and then. That way, they can see your positive changes—and, if any issues do arise later, you have a record of everything.

Leave no trace

If your landlord is uncooperative, your best options are containers, or growing annuals if you have access to open soil. They cannot quibble over short-lived plants or potted displays that you will take with you at the end of your tenancy. You never know, they may come around to your way of thinking—it's hard to make a property look worse by adding some greenery.

KEEP YOUR *landlord* IN THE LOOP

There are times when a conversation with your landlord about your garden is essential. Notes like this can be found throughout the book, highlighting when you should ask for prior approval or help from them.

Roommates, neighbors, and common spaces

A garden or terrace is a great place to gather people, especially in a shared house or apartment building. Before you start any new project, it's vital to include everyone who uses the space in the conversation.

Get talking

In my experience, communal outdoor spaces tend to be unloved because no one takes the initiative to improve them. So let everyone know what you're planning, either by creating a group on social media or dropping a friendly message in your neighbors' mailboxes. Tell them who you are and what you would like to do, and make it clear if you want ideas, help, or just a little freedom to improve the space. Ask them what they use the space for, if anything, and aim to ensure your plans would not hamper that. If a roof terrace is a favorite sunbathing spot in the summer, for example, filling it with trash cans

Gathering outdoors
Outdoor spaces are great for socializing. A small fire pit makes a good focus for a lazy evening.

turned into potato planters is not going to win you any friends. Share pictures of what you would like to do, or images of plants you'd like to grow, so people can get an idea of what you're planning.

Team effort

You might find that nobody else is interested in the garden, leaving you free to do as you please. Alternatively, your message may inspire others to get involved. Not only will this help lighten the workload, but by involving more people from the start, you're more likely to get your roommates or neighbors interested in taking care of the garden in the future. After all, people tend to want to look after the things they've helped create.

Agree a time to meet and discuss your ideas. It's all about keeping people informed and making it easy for them to say "yes" to your suggestions—as well as hearing any ideas they may have.

Accidents happen

You can't control everything that happens in a shared space: plants get trampled, pots get knocked over, balls end up where they shouldn't, and summer parties get livelier than expected. So avoid putting your best pots and plant displays in high-traffic areas where they could end up getting unpleasantly rearranged.

A place to eat
A simple set of tables and chairs adds another dimension to a small space.

Sharing a space
Communal gardens can be beautiful and offer somewhere to get together as well a peaceful sanctuary.

Making a plan

Transforming an outdoor space
does not need to be daunting.
By taking time to become familiar
with your space, and to figure out
how much time and money you
can give to it, you can start to
figure out exactly what you are
able to do. No matter your type
of space or length of lease,
it pays to have a plan before
you jump in.

Assessing your space

Before you do anything, spend time observing the space. Only by identifying exactly what you have to work with—the good, the bad, and the ugly—will you be able to make a decent plan.

Looking at what you have
Make a note of where the sun and shade fall at different times of day in your yard. Also try to identify existing plants to help you plan.

Reading the aspect

Take some time to get a feel for the space. With your back to your house or apartment, figure out in which direction you—and therefore your outdoor space—are facing. This is known as the "aspect," and will give you a good idea of where the sun will fall. If your space is predominantly north- or east-facing, expect shade for most of the day; if south- or west-facing, it will generally be sunnier. It's useful to know this so you can determine what kind of plants will thrive in your garden, as well as knowing where and when the sun will hit the elevation of the house (so you don't end up blocking sunlight through the windows with your plants). It'll also help you find the sunniest (or shadiest, if you prefer) space for a chair.

Weather and water watch

If you can, try to determine how weather will affect your garden. Buildings, walls, and trees might create "rain shadows," where rain is less likely to fall, or create areas that are more sheltered from high winds. This is all important to know when it comes to choosing the right plants for your space later.

If your yard has bare soil that you are planning to plant into, pick up a handful and give it a squeeze. If it crumbles easily, it will likely be on the sandy side, which means that water will drain through it faster. Clay soils, which will clump together when squeezed, are the opposite—they'll retain moisture longer.

Adopting existing plants

Your new garden may not be completely empty when you arrive. You may have inherited a hedge or some shrubs planted by the landlord, or some tired-looking container plants left by the last tenants. If the garden is looking tired or overgrown, you might be tempted to clear everything out and start again, but this isn't always a great tactic. What might look dull and uninteresting in winter might end up being your garden highlight in just a few months' time. It may also be hiding an unpleasant eyesore, so ripping it out may only make things look worse.

If you can, try and figure out what your inherited plants are. See if your landlord can tell you anything about them, or download a plant identifier app. If you know people who enjoy gardening, send them some photos—I know my friends and family never hold back with the "what am I?!" messages and I must admit I quite enjoy it.

> Even if you can't identify a mystery plant you've inherited, resist the urge to get rid of it if you can. Established plants can be a vital refuge for wildlife, and should be maintained wherever possible.

Working with what you have
An empty area such as a balcony
(left) can be filled with plants as you
wish. An existing tree (above) needs
more careful planning if you wish to
add plants around it.

Working with trees

Should you be lucky enough to find
yourself with a tree, make the most of
it because they tend to be few and far
between, especially in small urban
spaces. Think about how you can
plant around it—the area beneath the
tree's canopy will tend to be dry and
shady in summer, and lighter and
more open in winter (unless you have
an evergreen, in which case it will act
as a year-round screen for whatever is
on the other side).

Assets and eyesores

It can be hard to know where to start
when you take on a new space,
especially if it appears to have been
neglected for some time. You might
be quick to notice its flaws, but don't
let them distract you from the
potential. Take a moment to

Even if you can't figure out exactly
what a plant is, if it isn't dead or
diseased, resist the urge to get rid
of it. Established plants can also be a
vital refuge for wildlife, and should be
maintained wherever possible. I have
a top-heavy mass of ivy on my fence
that has gone years without a severe
prune and is forever alive with
sparrows, and I am very happy
with that.

KEEP YOUR *landlord* IN THE LOOP

If a tree is dominating the yard or blocking light getting into your plot,
it may need to be pruned. This is an expensive and intricate job, best handled
by a trained arborist in conversation with your landlord, so speak to them
rather than taking on this work yourself.

---

familiarize yourself with your new space: you might find that some of its features are assets in disguise, while others you may need to figure out how to live with. So, before you get going, take stock of what you see in front of you:

- **Existing plants** can be assets. Try to identify them and investigate how they'll grow. If they don't seem to have much merit, consider what kind of gap they'll leave if you remove them, as you might need to fill the hole they leave.
- **Abandoned decorative pots** or planters can often be cleaned or upcycled, giving them a second lease on life.
- **Litter, dead plants,** and broken items should be discarded right away—it always helps to look at a blank space without the distractions of detritus.
- **Gravel areas** can look grotty at first sight, but can be easily refreshed by dealing with any weeds (see pp.178–181) and topping up what's there with a few new bags of gravel matching what was already there.

- **Slippery paving** or decking needs the algae removed from it. You'll need a pressure washer for this, so look into a day's rental or ask your local online community if you can borrow one. This cleaning job will be time well spent.
- **Septic tanks,** fuel tanks, or ugly sheds will never be the highlight of any yard, so think about how you might screen these off. In the case of a shed, talk to your landlord about painting it. If you offer to do the work, your landlord may be more inclined to buy the stain or paint.

Seeing the potential

Don't be disheartened if everything isn't right on day one. In my rental garden, I inherited a collapsing fence and a rampant climber from my neighbor's garden. I pulled the fence back to its posts with cable ties, then battled the climber until my neighbor finally removed it. Neither were ideal but if I'd waited for both to be dealt with I would have had to put up with a horrible view for quite some time!

Spending and saving

When planning a garden, it's worth figuring out how much time and money you will realistically be able to spend on it. While limited time or money can initially feel like obstacles, by figuring out what is achievable, you can make the most of your resources—and your space.

Spending time

The more time you're willing to put into your garden, the more you will gain from it—but you can make a real difference even if your time is very short. Think about your typical weekly commitments. Will you be able to water a huge collection of potted plants week after week—and then sit in the garden afterward and appreciate your efforts? Will you be happy to wait for slow-growing plants to reach their potential if you only have a short-term lease?

The amount of time you'll need to spend maintaining your garden will mostly depend on the size and type of outdoor space you have. For instance, a lawn will need a lot more attention than a patio or other hard landscaping—although these will need occasional upkeep, too (see pp.150–151).

That being said, unless you happen to be renting acres of land, it's unlikely that you'll need to spend huge amounts of time taking care of the space. For an average-size urban garden, with a number of container plants and borders, I would estimate

a couple hours or so, twice a week, to tend to your plants during the summer months. Gardening, as a rule, often works better with the "little and often" approach, so as long as you don't neglect the garden for months on end the process should be more of a pleasure than a chore.

How much time you spend caring for your garden will also depend on the seasons (see pp.184–187). Spring is typically a busy time, when most of your work will involve setting up for the season ahead. This also marks the start of the growing season (April to September), when plants take advantage of the increased daylight hours. In the summer, you'll mainly be focusing on keeping your plants watered—during a heatwave, this could end up being a daily task. By the fall, you'll be left to tidy things up as the plants start to die off or become dormant. Once you reach the darker, winter months, you'll have very little to do to keep your dormant garden in good order—great news if you don't relish being outdoors in the cold!

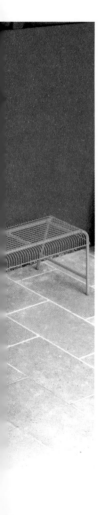

Planning ahead
Pot up slow-growing and costlier plants so that you can take them with you when you move, saving the beds for bulbs and other cheaper, quick-growing plants.

It's unlikely that you'll need to spend huge amounts of time taking care of your outdoor space. For an average-size urban garden, I would estimate a couple hours or so, twice a week, to tend to your plants during the summer months.

Spending and saving money

How much money you choose to spend on your garden will depend on many factors: how much disposable income you have, how long your tenancy agreement is, and how much time you're going to spend enjoying the garden once you've finished. Like many people, I find myself having good and bad months when it comes to money. Fortunately, gardens tend to need little investment around Christmas, which is when I usually find I'm without much disposable income.

Taste will play a huge role, too. While a number of gardeners will be happy growing tomatoes in growbags or upcycling tin cans to sow seed in, for others the priority will be to assemble a beautiful collection of good-quality containers and features. Personally, I'm happiest spending most of my budget on beautiful containers or slow-growing plants that I know will bring me years of enjoyment.

If you're not up for spending much cash, here are some tips that will help you on your way to creating the space you want:

- **Grow your plants from seed** (see pp.52–55). Packets of seeds often cost just a few pounds, making this a very cost-effective way of getting your garden underway.
- **Ask friends and family** to buy you gardening vouchers and other horticultural items for birthdays and other major occasions.
- **Check out local gardening groups** or online forums for plants that are either available for free or are available at a low price. Keep an eye out for seed swaps and giveaways in your neighborhood, too. I often leave seedlings on my front wall and they are snapped up within hours—one of the many pleasures of gardening is sharing.

Seasonal interest
This relaxed backyard (left) is used mainly in summer. The formal front yard (above) looks great all year.

Container creativity
Pots containing useful herbs make the most of these steps (left), while this wooden container is a focal point (above).

- **Stop by your nearest garden center** and ask if they have any spare plant pots you can take.
- **Be creative and save some empty containers** from your home. So long as they drain (meaning that they don't fill with water) most small containers can be upcycled into a plant pot.

Even if money is tight, there are a few key items you'll need to buy (or rent or borrow) to keep your garden looking at its best (see pp.38–39). Buy the best-quality potting mix you can afford for planting in containers—it will be an investment in the garden you're about to create. Don't forget to make use of a good mulch, either—it can help your garden look a lot more "finished," and is

Even if money is tight, it's worth spending as much as you can comfortably afford on good-quality tools and potting soil. Spending even a small amount of money on the garden always yields a great return on your investment—and that return is a great-looking space that will bring you pleasure and wellbeing.

extremely helpful if you want to avoid hours of weeding and keep your plants healthy (see p.179).

Overall, my advice is that spending even a small amount of money on the garden always yields a great return on your investment—and that return is a great-looking space.

Reimagining a space

If you have the chance to do so, it can be great fun to redesign your outdoor space. Even if you've never done it before and the task seems slightly daunting, think of it as an enjoyable creative challenge.

Any space—even a tiny or paved-over area—has the potential to be reimagined by a keen gardener who can see its possibilities. Garden design starts with simple doodling, so dig out a pad and pen and start jotting down some ideas.

Map out what you have

Start by measuring the dimensions and noting the position of any permanent features, such as sheds and trees. Use a simple scale, such as 1 in = 3 ft (2.5 cm = 1 m), so your proportions are right. Determine the aspect of your garden (see p.25) and see where north is. This will tell you which parts of your space will be in full sun, and which in shade—useful for placing items such as a seating area, or a spot for vegetables.

Redesigning a roof terrace
Would-be window boxes and other containers have been thoughtfully used to make the most of this small roof terrace.

Imagine what could be

Make a few copies of your garden plan, and use each one to try out a different combination of ideas. Do you want a bench in the sunniest corner, or would it be better by the back door? Could you hide eyesores with well-placed borders, or draw the eye away with a container display elsewhere? This is the time to be bold and let your imagination run wild—questions of cost or your landlord's approval will come later.

Mapping out what works

When you've settled on your preferred new layout, head into the space to see if it works. You can temporarily mark out your lines with a rope or a hose. Sometimes what looks great on paper may need adjusting, so make your changes in line with what feels right outside. If the space is long and thin, for example, narrow borders will draw your eye straight to the end, while more circular beds will stop the eye being drawn too quickly to the edges.

Once you have a rough layout you are pleased with, return to your paper plan and start adding planting ideas. It helps if you have an overall style in mind, such as a cottage or wildlife garden, or minimalist. To explore these styles, and the plants and materials that go with them, check out social media, gardening books, magazines, and TV programs.

Finalizing your plan

Once you have a sense of your new garden's layout and planting style, you can start to consider what furniture or lighting you might want (see pp.34–37).

Don't be deterred if you need to scale back the materials you want to use, or switch to more temporary options if your landlord isn't keen on permanent changes. Pots of bedding plants may give the impression of flowering borders, while paved paths can be replicated with bark chips. The trick is to identify what you really want, and what you're willing to compromise on in order to achieve it.

KEEP YOUR *landlord* IN THE LOOP

Discuss your proposals with your landlord, and not just to get permission—they may see you as a weekend garden designer without the fees and may be persuaded to pay for features, such as paths or better screening plants, which will enhance the value of their property in the long term.

Furniture

One of the joys of having an outdoor space is being able to relax in it. Whether this means relaxing in a chair with a book and a drink, or sitting around a table having a lazy weekend breakfast with friends, you might want some outdoor furniture.

Outdoor furniture can really add to the look and feel of a space by making it seem more inviting and cherished. Of course, you can just carry indoor furniture outside, but the chances are that you will be more inclined to linger for a few moments in your space if the furniture is already waiting for you. I think of furniture as an investment and look at it in the same way as, say, a centerpiece plant pot. If I can find the funds to buy something that looks good and is long-lasting, then I'll spend the money, knowing that I'll get pleasure from it for years.

Deciding what you need

Take a moment to think about how often you'll use your furniture, and what you're likely to use it for. After all, there is little point spending money

Dining in style
This elegant dining table forms a centerpiece in this sheltered city space.

on furniture that will take up precious space if you're not going to make the most of it.

For example, if you rarely have dinner parties, buying an enormous table with a set of eight chairs is probably not a good idea. In fact, you may not need a table at all: loose chairs or a bench can look equally inviting as the classic table-and-chairs set. In our home, I know my partner is more likely to be found on the moon than in the garden, no matter how beautiful it is, so I only made space for a chair and single table so I can relax there with a drink when I find time.

Material choices

Think carefully about what type of material you want your furniture to be made from. As well as affecting the visual appeal, different materials come with different practical considerations:

- **Wooden furniture** needs periodic maintenance—it's not difficult or demanding but if your yard is shady and damp, wood will rot quicker and grow algae. In a sunny space, wood such as oak and chestnut takes on an attractive silvery hue over time, and ages better.
- **Recycled composite plastic furniture** doesn't rot and can easily be wiped down.
- **Metal and cast-iron furniture** is a favorite of mine as it doesn't easily blow over, looks beautiful, and suits a variety of settings. However, it is heavy to move and cold to sit on without a cushion.
- **Rattan and cane furniture** can look great, but you'll need to store it indoors if it is to last. Some more modern takes on rattan are now produced in polyethylene, which is more robust in outdoor situations.

An inviting area
Seating and outdoor furniture transforms a space, creating an extension to the indoors.

Lighting

Adding ambient lighting can bring an element of magic after dusk and it's wonderful to be sitting outdoors on a summer evening in a lit space. In darker winter months, putting on the outdoor lights for a couple hours during the evening brings the space to life.

Like most things, lighting is subjective: the kind of lighting you wish to use, the amount, and even the color. Personally, I think it's hard to go wrong with warm whites and yellows, and I tend to avoid colored lights, as they remind me of Christmas decorations—not the look I'm aiming for!

Simplicity or impact?

A string of outdoor lights dotted through plants or worked through

Magical mood
Festoons of lights among the foliage give this small space an enchanting feel.

railings will give a sense of cheer, while solar-powered lights can make useful path markers. Neither of these lighting options will be powerful enough to light up entire garden features, but they can instantly deliver a wonderful atmosphere.

Choose festoon lighting if you want to actually light up your space for outdoor dining and living, as these strings of full-size light bulbs produce a surprising amount of light. To add a sense of depth and intrigue, you could even consider investing in small spotlights with adjustable heads, and positioning them so that they "uplight" trees, shrubs, or container displays. Try to arrange spotlights to that you don't see the source of the light itself—after all, no one wants the spotlight to fall directly in their line of sight.

Power sources

Most electric outdoor lighting options are easy to set up, but require a plug in a dry space, so if you don't

Light the way
Lanterns protect my plants' foliage from the heat of the candles inside, and protect the flames from gusts of wind.

have an outdoor weatherproof socket or a safe and secure way to plug the lights to an indoor socket, consider a plug-free alternative such as solar.

In addition to lights pre-fitted with solar panels, you can buy special kits with separate solar panels that can be located at a distance from the light source. That way, you can position your lights in a shady spot, while having the solar panel mounted in a sunnier place where it can charge up easily during the daytime.

Choosing and storing tools

People often worry that they need a full range of tools—and a shed to store them—before they start. There are a few essentials, but the list isn't as long as you might think.

When it comes to your budget, balance the amount you are able to spend on equipment with how much use, and therefore value, you're likely to get out of it in the space you have to garden.

Essential and handy tools

- **A watering can** is pretty essential. I like ones with a long spout so I can easily reach deep into my pot displays. Some also have a good "rain" or "rose" head attachment for watering seedlings and delicate young plants.
- **A spade or fork** is vital to dig up weeds and dead plants, especially in a larger area. If you store them outside, avoid ones with wooden handles, which are quicker to rot.
- **A trowel or hand fork** is another must-have for cultivating smaller areas and when planting bulbs.

The gardener's toolkit
By investing in the best-quality tools you can afford, you will be rewarded with items you can rely on for years to come.

- **A pruning saw** will deal with overgrown plants and shrubs, as well as more targeted pruning. A small folding saw is ideal.
- **A good pair of pruners** is useful in almost any garden. Some have a holster that you can clip to your belt. Pay for quality if you can, as you will use them for years to come.
- **A pair of hand shears** enables you to cut back wayward plants and to trim overgrown hedges.
- **Gardening gloves** protect your hands from prickly stems and leaves—and keep you warm in the winter!

Additional equipment

For bigger gardens, you might want to invest in a few extra tools (or ask your landlord if they are willing to supply them):

- **A hose** for when a watering can isn't enough to get the job done. It will need a suitable attachment for your outdoor or kitchen faucet. Hoses can be cumbersome to store, and may look ugly; I use an expandable black hose, which shrinks and drapes around my outside faucet when not in use. To avoid wasting water, make sure your hose is not left on, and check for leaks.
- **A hedge trimmer** is a quicker (if more expensive) alternative to hand shears, ideal for larger, more vigorous hedges. If you plan to invest in one, choose one with a rechargeable battery to avoid the hassle of cables.

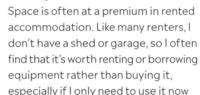

Pruning must-have
I recommend a small folding pruning saw if you need to keep shrubs and other woody plants in check (see pp.166-169).

Storage solutions

Space is often at a premium in rented accommodation. Like many renters, I don't have a shed or garage, so I often find that it's worth renting or borrowing equipment rather than buying it, especially if I only need to use it now and then. (The same is true for electric drills and other expensive tools that may only be used occasionally.)

When I'm buying hand tools, I tend to choose items made of recycled plastic rather than wood, so they can be left out all year without rotting, and I keep them under an evergreen shrub out of sight.

Space is often at a premium in rented accommodation. Like many renters, I do not have a shed or garage, so I often find that it's worth renting or borrowing equipment rather than buying it.

Quick fixes

If you're on a short lease (say,
a year or less), then gardening
displays that have near-instant
impact or are quick to put
together will be ideal for you. Try
out bedding plants for immediate
color, quick-growing climbers
and seeds, and container
combinations that you can take
with you to your next garden.

Instant planting

When you want a quick and easy flash of color,
bedding or annual plants can be a lifesaver. They are
inexpensive and sold everywhere from DIY stores
and nurseries to supermarkets and corner stores, and
offer an immediate burst of blooms.

Just like a tenant on a short-term
lease, bedding plants don't stick
around for long. They are typically
flowering annuals, which means that
they burst into life for one growing
season only, and are usually at their
peak in summer. By the fall, they will
start to die off, which is a natural part
of their life cycle—and it means that
you can make the most of their
colorful blooms without leaving
any valuable plants behind.

The ultimate gardening impulse
purchase, summer bedding plants
are found for sale in a wide variety
of stores from spring onward. Garden
centers and online stockists will give
you the best variety, but it doesn't
matter too much where you buy from
as long as the plants look fresh and
healthy. Avoid plants that have

Immediate impact
Pairing the bright colors of these
petunias with a contrasting pot
makes a bold, cheerful display.

Forming patterns
A mix of bedding plants repeated in this container makes a pretty, airy summer display.

dried-out soil, damaged stems, or diseased-looking leaves. Don't worry if they are not yet in flower at the time of purchase—it won't take long before they bloom.

Caring for annuals

Avoid planting out summer annuals too early in spring. Wait until the risk of frost has passed, as a sharp drop in temperature can damage or kill them. Otherwise, bedding plants are usually easy to please, and will thrive in containers or in beds and borders. They will happily provide plenty of

Bedding plants are usually easy to please, and will thrive in containers or in beds and borders. They will happily provide plenty of flowers through the summer if given adequate water.

flowers through the summer if they are given adequate water (see pp.162–165). To maximize their lifespan, feed them with slow-release fertilizer tablets or a regular liquid feed (see p.165). To extend the

flowering period, pinch off dead flowers weekly. This stops annuals from putting their energy into seed production, and instead prompts them to develop more blooms until the plants die down as frosts arrive.

Other bedding plants

Alongside flowering annuals (see pp.50–51), you might spot other plants sold as bedding plants, including shorter-lived perennials and tender shrubs such as French lavender and bergamot (*Monarda*). With a little care and attention (see pp.162–165), these may perform for a second summer.

Bedding plants for the fall and winter months are available, too, albeit a smaller selection: primroses, wallflowers, and colorful varieties of daisies (*Bellis perennis*) may all be available.

Bedding all year
Perennial grasses are used alongside bedding plants (above left) for a longer-lasting display. Pansies (below left) will last from fall and into spring.

Ringing the changes
A mixture of more permanent containers and some filled with summer bedding can make an area feel different in different seasons.

Just like a tenant on a short-term lease, summer bedding plants don't stick around for long. By the fall, they start to die off, which is a natural part of their life cycle—and it means that you can make the most of their colorful blooms without leaving any valuable plants behind for the next tenants.

Project
Instant crate display

This inexpensive and easy project can be planted up in minutes, with a repurposed wooden crate and fabric liner providing a great way to show off some colorful bedding plants.

You will need

- **Wooden packing crates**, ideally in different sizes
- **Old fabric** to line the crates
- **Potting mix**
- **Scissors** to trim the fabric
- **Slow-release fertilizer granules**
- **A selection of bedding plants** (see pp.50–51 for ideas)
- **Decorative mulch** (optional)
- **Empty pots or bricks** to raise up some of the crates (optional)

While packing crates are not conventional plant pots, they can be a great option for a short-lived summer display. You can find them in housewares and interior shops, or garden centers. If your rental circumstances change during the summer, they are light enough to be transported easily to your new location while still being sturdy enough not be blown over by summer storms!

When selecting bedding plants for this project, limit yourself to one or two types of bedding plant per crate to avoid a piecemeal look. If you can, try to stick to a consistent color theme for each crate, too; this will give your display a confident, purposeful look that contrasts well with the informality of the crates. For this project, I chose double-flowered primroses (*Primula*) for the smallest crate, while the medium-size crate showcases single-flowered primroses with a double-flowered daffodil (*Narcissus*, see p.104) peeking through. In the largest crate, I used white bellflowers (*Campanula*).

Creating a long-lasting display

In order to prevent potting mix falling through the slats, and water draining away before it can be taken up by the plants' roots, you need to line your crates. While you could use purpose-made material, such as hanging basket liner, reusing old clothing or carpet scraps offers a sustainable option—I cut up an old fleece jacket to line my crates. If your choice of material is waterproof, remember to make some holes in it to ensure that excess water can drain away.

Adding height

If all your crates are the same size, use old terra-cotta pots or bricks to raise a few of them up to different heights and create a more eye-catching display.

Sun lovers
For a more drought-tolerant display, choose succulent plants such as *Echeveria* and *Haworthia*. Often sold as houseplants, they cope well in full sun over the summer months.

How to create it

Place the liner fabric into the crate. Make sure you have plenty of excess; don't trim it back just yet. If using waterproof material, snip a few holes in the bottom to provide drainage.

Mix in slow-release fertilizer granules in line with the product's application instructions. Bedding plants exhaust potting mix in 4–6 weeks, so adding fertilizer really helps prolong the display.

2

Fill the crates almost to the top with potting mix, leaving a 1in (2.5cm) gap for watering.

3

Trim the fabric down to the potting mix level, so the liner is not visible.

5

Plant the annuals in the crates, close enough that they just touch, and fill the container. Lightly firm the potting mix around the plants.

6

Water the plants in well, making sure to direct the water toward the roots. Place the crates in a sunny area, arranging them at different heights if preferred (see opposite). Water once or twice a week.

Get started with …
Plants for instant color

When you're only renting a place for a short amount of time, buying pre-grown bedding plants makes it easy to create an instant, high-impact display. Don't get too hung up on specific varieties here—just remember to check the label to make sure they'll suit the growing conditions of your outdoor space.

1 Begonias

☀ ◐: tuberous types to 18 in (45 cm); annual types 6-8 in (15-20 cm)

These great performers come in two types. Tuberous varieties (*shown*) tend to have green leaves and large flowers, while annual types (*Begonia semperflorens*) have smaller, more profuse blooms and, depending on the variety, may also have deep red leaves.

2 Busy Lizzie (*Impatiens*)

☼ ☽ 8–12 in (20–30 cm)

A favorite, busy Lizzies are compact and flower reliably, even in part shade. Look for the New Guinea hybrids, which have a darker red flush to their otherwise green foliage.

3 French lavender (*Lavandula stoechas*)

☼ 12–16 in (30–40 cm)

Less hardy than its English cousin, French lavender is often sold as summer bedding. It has elegant flowers and a wonderful scent.

4 Pansy (*Viola*)

☼ ☽ 6–8 in (15–20 cm)

Available in a range of colors from yellows to purple and even black, these rewarding, fast-growing annuals have the bonus of edible flowers.

5 Nemesia

☼ to 6 in (15 cm)

Nemesia make an easy addition to any summer display. Look out for the 'Wisley Vanilla' cultivar, which has a delicious scent.

6 Petunia

☼ upright types 12 in (30 cm); trailing types 4 in (10 cm)

With trumpetlike blooms in striking colors, petunias come in both trailing and upright varieties.

7 Lobelia

☼ ☽ to 30 in (15 cm)

Commonly found in shades of blue, white, and mauve, lobelias have masses of small flowers. They're great for spilling over container edges.

8 Pelargonium

☼ ☽ to 16 in (40 cm)

Sometimes incorrectly labeled as geraniums, these are a reliable choice. Remove spent flower heads for the best results.

Growing from seed

Raising annual flowers from seed is a cost-effective way of creating lots of summer color. It doesn't take too long, and if you start the process off early indoors, you can be ready with plenty of seedlings to plant outside once the weather warms up. It's great fun watching them grow, too.

By sowing annual seed in late winter or early spring, you can usually expect to see blooms by summer. Many of these plants will go on to produce seed and then die by the end of the season, so you can happily commit to planting in beds and borders in the knowledge that you'll not be leaving much-loved plants behind when your short-term lease runs out.

Choosing seeds

When buying seed, always read the back of the packet or the description in the seed catalog to note the growing advice. For example, some seeds enjoy lots of exposure to light while others need a few weeks in the fridge before they will germinate.

There are often more seeds in a packet than you will need—the odd seedling is commonly lost to slugs and snails and some may not germinate successfully. The packet usually indicates a rough number of plants you can expect. If you find yourself with spares, you can give them away to friends or neighbors.

Always check the "sow by" date on the packet. While many seeds can grow after this date, old seed may not germinate as well.

The basics

GROWING ANNUALS FROM SEED

01
Fill your pots or tray with seed starting mix, firm down gently to create a flat surface, and water lightly. Sow the seed, then cover with more starting mix (if necessary).

Annuals in a border
Tall, salmon-pink snapdragons (*Antirrhinum*) are annuals that are easy to grow from seed. Here, they are growing among dahlias and an annual blue salvia.

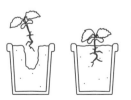

02
When the seedlings have developed their first pair of true leaves, gently transplant them into individual pots to grow on.

03
When all risk of frost has passed, move the remaining young plants outdoors to harden off, before being planted into their final positions.

Starting seedlings indoors

The packet will tell you whether your seed can be sown, or "started off," under cover. Sowing indoors lets you get a head start on spring, by protecting tender seedlings from any late frosts and ensuring you have seedlings ready to plant when the weather warms up.

In early spring (or whenever the packet specifies), fill a seed tray or container with seed starting mix. You can buy seed starting mix, or break up standard potting mix to remove any lumps. Gently firm the mix down to create an even surface, then water lightly. Sow the seeds according to packet instructions: some will need covering with a further layer of starting mix, while others can just be scattered on the surface.

Cover with a clear plastic lid, or push a few small sticks into the soil and put a clear food bag over the top. This ensures that the starting mix does not dry out. Air this out daily so it does not become stagnant inside, and remove it once germination occurs. Place on an east- or west-facing windowsill, watering as needed so the starting mix does not dry out.

Once the seeds have developed their first full pair of leaves, carefully transplant the strongest-looking ones into small pots or "plug trays,"

> There are often more seeds in a packet than you will need—the odd seedling is commonly lost to slugs and snails and some may not germinate successfully.

handling them by their leaves. Let them grow in their same position on the windowsill for another 2–3 weeks.

Plants started off indoors may need a period of "hardening off," or acclimating them to the outside so that the exposure does not shock and kill them. To do this, place them outdoors in a sheltered position (for example, at the base of a sunny wall) for around two weeks. Do not move them outside until all risk of frost has passed; if a late cold snap takes you by surprise, move tender seedlings back under cover to protect them.

Planting out young plants

Before you plant your seedlings outside, you need to prepare the area. The best results are gained in a sunny spot. Fork over the top 6–12 in (15–30 cm) and add some nutrients. I like using pelleted chicken manure as it's easy to handle and readily available.

Plug plants

If you don't relish the idea of raising plants from seed, you can buy young seedling "plugs" of annual plants from catalogs or nurseries. These are young plants that you can grow on and transplant into their final positions as you would with homegrown seedlings (see left).

Sowing outdoors

If you don't have space indoors or if you want to start the process a little later, you can sow the seeds directly into open ground. Depending on packet instructions, you'll likely need to wait until late spring, or whenever your soil temperature has warmed up and the risk of frost has passed. Keep a sharp eye out for slugs and snails.

Growing on and transplanting
Here, old cardboard tubes have been reused as pots for sowing (left). When seedlings have several leaves and are growing strongly (above), they can be transplanted to grow on.

Get started with …
Annuals from seed

Summer-flowering annuals are a fun, easy, and affordable way of adding quick-growing flower power to your garden, either in open ground or in containers. Raised from seed in the spring and planted out after the last frost has passed, they perform through the summer until the frosts arrive.

1 **Cosmos**
(*Cosmos bipinnatus*)
:☼: :☼: to 39 in (100 cm)

With airy, fernlike foliage and showy white or pink flowers in summer, cosmos are hugely impactful. Pinch out the growing tip when they are 12 in (30 cm) tall.

2 Spanish flag (*Ipomoea lobata*)

☼ to 16 ft (5 m)

Perhaps one of the prettiest climbers to grow from seed, this has red, yellow, and orange all present on the same flower, aging to white at the base of the flower. Position it in heat and sun.

3 Love-lies-bleeding (*Amaranthus caudatus*)

☼ ☼ to 20 in (50 cm)

This is a curious plant with striking, pendant, dark red flowers.

4 Nasturtium (*Tropaeolum majus*)

☼ ☼ to 8 in (20 cm)

Flowers are yellow, orange, or red, and some types have white-splashed leaves. It's great for scrambling or trailing, and the flowers are delicious in salads.

5 Annual baby's breath (*Gypsophila elegans*)

☼ to 12 in (30 cm)

A cottage garden classic, this is known for blooming into clouds of tiny white flowers.

6 Woodland tobacco plant (*Nicotiana sylvestris*)

☼ ☼ to 4 ft (1.2 m)

For evening scent and height in a border, these nodding, trumpetlike white flowers are an elegant option.

7 Love-in-a-mist (*Nigella damascena*)

☼ to 12 in (30 cm)

The flowers of these annuals, typically blue or white, can be spied in early to midsummer through a haze of delicate foliage.

8 Spider flower (*Cleome hassleriana*)

☼ to 3 ft (1 m)

These unusual-looking annuals love heat and sunshine, making them a perfect choice for warm spaces.

Container planting

For gardeners with limited space or no open soil, containers are the way to go. As well as being portable to take with you when you leave, potted plants can have a real wow factor and, in a small space, allow you to easily change your display at any time of year.

Container displays can often be regarded as inferior to "traditional" forms of gardening—the second-best option when nothing else will work. I disagree. My whole garden is made up of pots, which I've carefully arranged to create an impact (see right).

Choosing the right containers

Drainage holes are essential in any plant pot; otherwise, the roots will quickly become waterlogged and the plant will become susceptible to rot. It's also important to think about the stability of your containers, especially on roof terraces and balconies, which can often be blustery spaces. Consider buying square-bottomed pots rather than round ones, which are less likely to blow over.

Caring for container plants

Plants in pots need a little more attention than they would otherwise require if they were planted in the ground. Since their roots have access to less soil, they need to be watered more often, and may need additional feeding (see p.165).

They also need to be supported to prevent them falling over. When planting up new pots, add a brick or gravel in the base to give them extra weight. Arrange them close together so they can support one another. On balconies and in other exposed sites, consider securing taller pots at the rear of the display to railings.

Arranging containers

There are some simple steps you can take to maximize the visual impact of your container displays:
• **Think about the backdrop.** A hedge, wall, or fence will provide a

My container garden
As I have a fairly small space, all paved, containers create a vibrant display with plenty of visual interest.

Grouping containers
A collection of succulents in colorful containers stands out against a dark fence (top), while this mass of flowering spring bulbs (above) packs a punch all together.

sense of height and depth—and will also offer shelter.

- **Go big.** It might seem counterintuitive, but the addition of a few large plants will not only have a great impact in a small space but can often make that space feel larger.

- **Choose your focal point.** This could be one eye-catching plant positioned in the center of the display, or a particularly appealing-looking pot. In my garden, the containers are all arranged around a water feature (see p.59).

- **Fill in the display** by placing small and medium-size plants around your focal plant. Use them to hide any less-attractive containers nearer the back of the display, and to plug any gaps in the arrangement.

Containers center stage
A group of foliage plants in containers in the alcove makes an eye-catching feature. Larger plants in pots provide movement and soften the lines of the seating area.

Get started with …
Container plants for structure

The suggestions below can all happily live in pots for years, if supplied with enough water and nutrients (see pp.162–165). They bring structure, form, and the all-important "bones" to a container display, providing a visual foil to flowering plants. Some will grow quickly, providing impact from day one, while others may take years to grow to their full potential.

1 Palms
☀ ☀ Growth speed: slow

For architectural shape and form, palms are a great choice. Look for *Chamaerops* (shown), *Butia*, or *Trachycarpus*. Cabbage palm (*Cordyline*) is not a true palm but gives a similar feel and is faster-growing and more affordable.

2 Bay tree
(*Laurus nobilis*)
☀ ☀ Growth speed: fast

An evergreen providing year-round shape and form, the bay is perfect as a backdrop and handy in the kitchen.

3 Evergreen ferns
☀ ☀ Growth speed: medium

Evergreen ferns such as *Asplenium*, *Blechnum* (shown), and *Polypodium*, are, useful in the shadier parts of the garden.

4 Bamboo

☼ ☽ ☀ Growth speed: medium

Quick-growing bamboo offers plenty of height to screen eyesores. While their roots are known for spreading quickly and causing problems if planted into beds, it will be fine in a thick-sided pot where it can be safely contained.

5 Castor oil plant (*Fatsia japonica*)

☽ ☀ Growth speed: medium

These evergreens brighten up shady corners with their winter flowers and small fruits. The 'Spider's Web' cultivar is a favorite of mine.

6 Sedges (*Carex*)

☼ ☽ Growth speed: fast

Evergreen *Carex* comes in shades of green, silver, and gold variegation.

7 Succulents

☼ Growth speed: slow

Many succulents are cold tolerant in a sheltered spot. *Aloe* (shown), *Echeveria*, and *Agave* are all great for a sunny pot display—but you may need to bring them indoors over winter.

8 Pittosporum

☼ ☽ Growth speed: fast

A useful filler, these evergreens quickly form a colorful backdrop.

Climbers

Climbing plants are ideal for rental gardeners on short leases. With the right variety of climber, you can easily and effectively hide eyesores, support wildlife, and add an extra burst of color and greenery to even the smallest of spaces.

As their name suggests, climbers grow up and up, using twining stems, suckers, or other features to attach themselves to nearby supports. In nature, they scramble up trees and shrubs in order to soak up the sun. Gardeners have long used this trick for their own benefit. By training climbers against designated structures (such as bamboo canes, trellis, or even walls), they can be used to hide unappealing eyesores or soften the appearance of bare spaces.

Choosing climbers

Before you buy any climbing plant, find out how fast it is likely to grow. Some, such as the mile-a-minute vine (*Fallopia baldschuanica*), spread with an almost alarming vigor and, when planted in the wrong place, can become a menace, heading for your neighbors' gardens after swamping your own! These have given climbers a reputation for damaging walls and other structures.

While some climbers are best avoided, many varieties, such as those shown on pp.72–73, will be perfectly well behaved in your garden.

Providing support

How you support your climber will depend on the way in which it climbs. Most can be divided into two types: twining climbers, such as jasmine, *Stauntonia*, or *Clematis*, and self-sticking varieties, which include Virginia creeper (*Parthenocissus*) and ivy (*Hedera*). Twining climbers do better on wires and trellis panels, while the self-sticking do better against flat walls and fences.

There is also a large group of roses, known as "climbers and ramblers," that need some sort of framework to attach to, such as wires or trellises. These don't do well if left to their own devices and need pruning and training periodically.

Vertical gardening
When you want to make the most of the space in your yard, you can clothe the walls with climbers for a lush effect.

Focal point
In a small space, choosing an attractive support is almost as important as finding the right climber.

Growing climbers

Often quick-growing plants, climbers need maintaining little and often during the growing season. Be sure to tie or weave in new shoots to supports or trellises, or else they will wrap around each other or latch onto the nearest plant instead. Whatever kind of climber you have, it's worth checking up on their particular pruning requirements as soon as you can. If you do nothing with them for several months, you'll have a tangle to sort out!

Using climbers for screening

If you have an eyesore in your yard that you need to screen, climbers are an ideal solution. Depending on your circumstances, you could install a trellis panel with your landlord's permission, or else create a few tripods for container-planted climbers (see pp.68–71) and position them where they can disguise the eyesore. Make sure to use an evergreen climber, such as star jasmine (*Trachelospermum*), to ensure year-round coverage.

KEEP YOUR *landlord* IN THE LOOP

Landlords may not be too keen on the idea of having vigorous, unruly climbers, especially if they are left behind after you move on. To reassure them, only plant slower-growing varieties in beds and borders, so the next tenants aren't left to prune away masses of growth each year.

Making a wall into a feature
A plain wall painted a bold color
can become a striking feature. Here, the
fast-growing annual climber black-eyed
Susan (*Thunbergia alata*) twines round
its supports.

Project
Clematis tripod

With just a container, three hazel branches, and a climbing plant, you can quickly bring height and drama to a space, and create a focal point that provides both color and scent to your garden.

Climbing plants are not just utilitarian subjects, useful for screening eyesores (see p.66). Their wonderful flowers and scents can evoke powerful sensory memories: the evening perfume of honeysuckle, the summer abundance of climbing roses, or the sight of billowing fountains of wisterias in full bloom.

If your landlord isn't keen on having a climbing plant scramble up along walls, or you want a way to enjoy climbers without having to leave them behind at the end of your tenancy, a tripod in a pot is the way to go. Due to their often-vigorous nature, it takes no time at all for a young climber to fill out this simple wooden frame, making them ideal for the most impatient of gardeners (like me!). Many garden centers sell climbers already secured to tall canes or trellis supports, but it takes no time at all to upgrade this look and create a rustic display that you can easily take with you when the time comes for you to move on.

You will need

- **Large, heavy pot,** such as terra-cotta or metal, that can comfortably hold support poles
- **Potting mix**
- **Slow-release fertilizer**
- **A climbing plant** (see pp.72-73 for ideas)
- **3-4 wooden supports,** at least 6½ ft (2 m) long, such as hazel branches or bamboo canes
- **Twine or string**

Planning your climber display

For this project, I've used a *Clematis montana*, but you could try a variety of climbers, including annuals and perennials. For something like a *Clematis*, one plant per pot is enough; for smaller annuals, such as sweet peas, you'll need three or four plants, one for each wooden support.

Hazel branches are best for this project as the rough, twiggy surface provides more support for the plant to twine around and hold onto. If you can't find those, any sturdy branch or bamboo cane can be used instead.

Climber care

Many climbers have brittle stems, and one fracture could cause the loss of all growth beyond the break. Be careful when unfastening stems from an existing support, and again when training the stems onto the new tripod—don't tie the string too tight.

Removing existing supports
Carefully remove the climber from the canes it was sold with, cutting away any ties or straps.

How to create it

1

Fill the pot with the potting mix and add in a generous amount of slow-release fertilizer. Climbers are hungry plants, and this will help achieve quick results.

5

Insert the supports (3 or 4, depending on the size of the pot) at equal points around the edge. They should lean outward as much as possible, as this makes a wider tripod when you tie the tops together.

2 Once the climber is free of the support it came with (see opposite), gently untangle the stems as best you can.

3 Carefully remove the climber from its original pot, and plant it into the new container.

4 Pack fresh potting mix into any gaps around the sides of the container, then lightly firm the climber into place with your fingers.

6 Pull the tops of the supports together, and bind them securely with string or wire.

7 Carefully wrap the stems around the supports, occasionally securing loosely with a little string. Wind in as many stems as you can lower down the tripod—the climber will naturally want to race skyward as it grows.

8 Water well and place the pot in a position suitable for your chosen climber. The climber should begin to fill out the tripod in just a few weeks.

Get started with …
Climbing plants

The sheer number of climbing plants on offer can be quite overwhelming, especially if you are in a large garden center and find yourself among the clematis, of which there are countless varieties. Start by narrowing down whether you would like an evergreen or deciduous type, then consider which flower color you're looking for. Check how fast the climber grows, too.

1 *Clematis armandii*
:☼: **Growth speed: medium**

This evergreen clematis is adorned with white flowers in spring. so it's great at livening up a wall or fence, rather than acting as a dense screen. Needs wires or trellis.

2 Ivy (*Hedera*)
☀ Growth speed: medium

Available in all leaf shapes and sizes, ivy is an excellent screening plant that clings to walls or fences without support. Its late summer flowers are also a great nectar source for pollinators.

3 Star jasmine (*Trachelospermum jasminoides*)
☀ Growth speed: medium

Scented, white summer flowers and red-flushed winter foliage. Needs wires or trellis.

4 *Clematis montana*
☀ Growth speed: fast

A spring-flowering deciduous clematis, this has white, cream, or pink blooms. Needs wires or trellis.

5 Common jasmine (*Jasminum officinale*)
☀ Growth speed: medium

Hard to beat for perfume, this jasmine grows well in mild, sheltered gardens. Needs wires or trellis.

6 *Rosa banksiae* 'Lutea'
☀ Growth speed: fast

This thornless rose can reach a significant size, so suits larger spaces. Needs wires or trellis.

7 Small-leaved Virgina creeper (*Parthenocissus tricuspidata* 'Veitchii')
☀ Growth speed: medium

A deciduous climber with unbeatable fall color, this is self-clinging and can climb most structures.

8 *Ipomoea* 'Heavenly Blue'
☀ Growth speed: fast

An annual climber that can be raised from seed, it offers trumpet-shaped blue flowers. Needs wires or trellis.

Settling in

When your lease stretches to a
year or two, you'll know what to
expect from your garden as the
seasons come around again.
Putting in a little more time and
effort in the first year—planting
bulbs that will pop up to surprise
you months later, greening up
walls and windowsills, or even
trying your hand at growing your
own produce—will pay off
handsomely in the second.

Using window boxes

Window boxes are a wonderful way to bring color and life to otherwise unused spaces. They are a glimpse of the occupier's taste in plants—and their personality, too! If they are facing the street, window boxes bring pleasure to both passers-by and those living indoors.

Window boxes fit best on properties with windows that offer a deep external windowsill, and on windows where the lower half can open to make watering and feeding easy. This design is most common in older properties; where I live in London, for instance, I'm near many Victorian and Edwardian houses, so window boxes are a common sight.

Woven window boxes
These boxes are filled with a limited color range of white and green to beautiful effect.

The basics

HOW TO MOUNT WALL BRACKETS

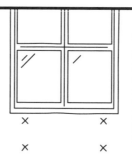

01
Check the wall area for any hidden utilities such as pipes or wires (it would be unusual to find these under a window). Measure and mark the holes where the brackets will be drilled into place.

More modern houses often don't have windowsills, which can make window boxes more of a challenge. If you're in this situation, don't give up on the idea, as you may be able to install wall brackets to fit a window box beneath your window (see below). Even if an under-window display isn't an option, window boxes themselves can be used in all sorts of unusual spaces: on top of low walls, or even on one end of wide steps (assuming the whole width isn't required for access).

Keeping things secure

If your window box is above the ground floor, you'll need to consider what lies below—you won't be popular with your downstairs neighbors if you end up soaking their washing when you're watering your plants. Likewise, if your window box overlooks a busy street or path it will be a hazard if it slips off. To reduce the risk of this happening, use wall brackets (see below), choose a heavier box such as stone or terra-cotta, which will be far less likely to blow off, and avoid using tall plants that could catch the wind (they would look too big for the display, anyway).

KEEP YOUR *landlord* IN THE LOOP

As brackets need to be drilled directly into the external wall, check with your landlord that they approve of what you're doing.

Planning your planting

I'm often surprised to see what people successfully grow in their window boxes. Sometimes plants have started life indoors before being ejected outside! By the nature of where they are placed, window boxes benefit from being more sheltered than other container displays, allowing you to choose less hardy plant varieties if you wish.

When choosing what to plant, remember to consider the direction, or "aspect," of your window (see p.25).

02
Using an electric drill and a suitable drill bit, make the required holes. Insert anchors, then attach the brackets to the wall firmly with screws.

03
Carefully slide or drop the planted-up window box into the cradle-like space created by the brackets, making sure that it will take the weight of the display when it is fully watered.

Colorful displays
A mix of violas (right) makes a cheerful window box for spring. A variety of foliage colors (below right) adds to the impact of this window box.

On a south-facing aspect, which faces the sun for much of the day, a window box will get baked and will likely need regular watering (see pp.162–165), whereas on a north-facing aspect the reverse will be true—in the winter, a north-facing box will receive very little sunshine and may even freeze. East- and west-facing windows are a little more moderate.

You may have little choice about the aspect of your window box, but you can select plants that will thrive in the conditions there. The suggestions on pp.84–85 show whether the plants thrive in sun or shade. For other plants, check the labels for their preferred conditions.

Adding height
This large window has space for
a mix of tall lupins, cosmos, and
antirrhinums, creating a cottage
garden in a window box.

Project
Sunny succulent window box

Whether your windowsills are the only outdoor spaces you have available to plant up, or you want to start with something easy before embarking on the yard, this simple weekend project is small-scale gardening at its best.

You will need

- A window box
- Hand drill (optional)
- Cactus potting mix
- Slow-release fertilizer
- Selection of succulents (or other plants to suit your window's light levels)
- Decorative gravel mulch
- Wall brackets (optional)

While much of the joy of gardening comes from spending time outdoors among your plants, in reality most of us will spend more time inside our homes, looking out at our greenery. Window boxes bridge that gap, by bringing plants right up to our windows where we can easily appreciate them, while also providing a welcome sight to any passers-by.

I like to treat my windowsills as if they were part of a picture frame, and imagine what my plants will look like from the inside as well as the outside. If space allows, I also like to add a single pot at either end of each window box, to give a little extra height to the display and create a more of a "garden scene."

As shown in this project, succulents are the ideal choice for south-facing windowsills, which tend to get a lot of sun. If your sills are a little more shaded, feel free to mix up the planting with more suitable alternatives—in addition to those shown on pp.84–85, many container plants (see pp.62–63) and even a few bulbs (see pp.104–105) would work nicely, as long as they suit the light conditions of your chosen windowsill.

Planning your window boxes

Make sure to measure your windowsill before choosing and planting your box. You want a box narrow enough that it will not overhang the edge of the sill, while also tall enough that you'll be able to comfortably see your plants from the inside as well as the outside. Windowsills can be surprisingly low, making smaller plants harder to see when indoors, so aim to include at least one large centerpiece plant that will draw the eye. If your windowsill slopes away from the window, use slivers of wood or doorstops to level the box.

Sunny swap
This alternative sun-loving display uses pink *Sedum*, white *Bacopa*, and silver *Helichrysum*.

How to create it

1

If your window box does not have drainage holes in the base, carefully drill several evenly spaced holes into it.

4

Working from the front edge of the box, arrange the remaining plants, tilting them slightly forward so they are clearly visible.

2 Fill the box close to the top with potting mix and mix in some of slow-release fertilizer in line with the product application instructions.

3 Select your largest plant, which will be the centerpiece of the display. Plant this in the middle of the box. Add any other large plants on either side.

5 Once the box is fully planted, cover any open soil with a decorative gravel or mulch.

6 Water the box thoroughly, then position it on the windowsill or within the wall brackets, if used (see pp.76–77).

Get started with …
Window box plants

The best plants for window boxes are happy with confined roots, tolerant of
challenging locations, and have a trailing habit to tumble over the edges of
the box. Taller plants are less suitable as they may block the view from the
window, or make the window box unstable in windy weather.

1 *Sedum sieboldii*
'Mediovariegatum'
☼ to 4 in (10 cm)
This delightful trailing
succulent has blue and
yellow leaves, followed
by pink flowers in late
summer. Position
along the front edges
of a window box to
display the stems
to the best effect.

**2 Houseleek
(Sempervivum)**
☼ to 4 in (10 cm)
Sempervivum species
and cultivars have
cute rosettes of
succulent leaves in
shades of green, rusty
brown, and red.

**3 Silverbush
(Convolvulus
cneorum)**
☼ to 12 in (30 cm)
This small evergreen
shrub combines
glossy silver leaves
with white flowers in
spring and summer.

4 Digger's speedwell (*Parahebe perfoliata*)

☼ to 12 in (30 cm)

This evergreen perennial has purple flowers in late summer against waxy blue leaves, formed curiously around the trailing stems.

5 Blechnum ferns (*Blechnum*)

☼ 6–12 in (15–30 cm)

Species and cultivars of *Blechnum* are lovely, often evergreen, ferns with coppery colored young fronds.

6 Spurge (*Pachysandra*)

☼ to 6 in (15 cm)

Pachysandra species and cultivars are evergreens suited to shade and will billow over the sides of a window box.

7 Ivy-leaved cyclamen (*Cyclamen hederifolium*)

☼ to 4 in (10 cm)

A fall-flowering perennial, this copes with dry shade.

8 *Ophiopogon planiscapus* 'Nigrescens'

☼ to 4 in (10 cm)

This evergreen offers wonderful black leaves with small clusters of lilac summer flowers and sometimes berries.

Planting in odd spaces

Sometimes our outdoor spaces are not the traditional ones we imagine—borders store trash cans, lawns are concrete, and the only access to soil is a narrow strip along the bottom of the fence. Thankfully, spaces of all shapes and sizes provide opportunities for planting.

Never underestimate the power of small or awkward spaces. When you have little room to create your perfect garden, every gap, crevice, and section of wall or fence is an opportunity. If you're unsure where to start, just watch the weeds: if they can thrive in the odd little corners of your space, so can your plants!

Planting in the gaps

Even if your space is entirely paved over, there may be opportunities to green it up without solely relying on containers. A shallow layer of sand and grit dusted between paving stones can be enough to sustain some plants, including the daisylike Mexican fleabane (see p94).

In my own yard, the cracks in the paving were full of bitter cress, and

Breaking up paving

In a paved area, it may be possible to take advantage of any loose slabs, with permission from your landlord, lifting them to make room for plants.

the strip along the bottom of the fence was riddled with dandelions. I have since swapped them for clusters of lace aloe (*Aloe aristata*) along the fence base, and fluffy green lines of mind-your-own-business (*Soleirolia soleirolii*) between the paving, and I'm much happier with the result.

In the smallest of gaps, it might not be possible to insert an actual plant. Instead, brush some seeds into the gaps and see if they take hold. Remember to water them in dry spells, as the limited root space will mean that they may need some extra help in order to thrive.

Vertical gardening

Not everyone has ample outdoor space. Narrow yards and balconies can quickly fill up with containers, leaving little room for anything else. The solution, in spaces like these, is simple: grow up.

The easiest way to add vertical greenery is with a climbing plant (see pp.64–67) secured to the wall with trellis or other simple supports, such as a series of horizontal wires spaced 12 in (30 cm) apart. A green wall structure (see pp.90–93) is a bigger investment (of both time and money), but pays off with an even bigger wow factor.

Greening a dark corner
Here, space and light are in short supply. A green wall grows up from a dark basement to the floor above, while a raised planter brings foliage into the light.

Scented path
Thymes add both color and scent
to this walkway. These plants
thrive in full sun and poor soil.

Planting on a wall
A tapestry of succulents creates a picture-like effect for this sunny wall.

Beyond the garden

The more you look for unusual places to add a little greenery, the more you can find. Stray beyond the limits of your rented property and you may spot a few guerrilla gardening opportunities in your local area, in spaces that are crying out for a little extra color and attention.

One great example of this is planting up the spaces beneath street trees using cheap bedding plants or surplus homegrown seedlings. With just a small patch of open soil, you can create a rewarding and much-loved feature in your neighborhood to be enjoyed by passers-by and pollinators alike. Choose plants with flexible stems that will cope with the odd stray footstep, such as geraniums—I once underplanted a local street tree with *Geranium* 'Rozanne' to great effect.

Spreading color around
Adding low-growing, fairly compact plants around a local street tree brings color and variety to your area. Here a dwarf *Ceanothus* adds a splash of blue to the tree base.

Project
Green wall

Where outdoor space is limited—say, a long and narrow yard or a tiny balcony—vertical gardening allows you to maximize your growing space and green up blank, boring walls.

Green walls are usually made up of pouches or compartments that attach to a wall, to which you can add potting mix and plants. At its simplest, a green wall can be a reclaimed wooden pallet lined with recycled plastic sheeting to create planting pockets, but you can also buy premade structures, some of which even have their own watering systems to keep plants at their best. The modular structure I have used in this project is made from recycled plastic, and is sturdy enough that it could easily be moved between gardens at the end of a tenancy.

While the growing space in each green wall compartment is quite small, and the soil space quite limited, do not underestimate the weight of it all when fully planted and watered. Because of this, green walls are best attached to brick walls only, although very small systems could conceivably be attached to the strongest of fences. Consult with your landlord before attaching a green wall, and remember to refill screw holes with mortar if the structure is removed when you move out.

You will need

· A wall or sturdy fence
· A green wall kit with recommended screws and anchors
· Electric drill
· Hammer
· Potting mix
· A selection of shallow-rooted, low-growing plants

Choosing your plants

A huge variety of different plant types can be used to populate your green wall. In this project, I've combined ferns, grasses, and trailing ivies with the purple foliage of *Tradescantia* 'Nanouk' to create a display with a range of colors and textures. These plants are ideally suited to the shady conditions of this narrow, sheltered space. For sunnier spots, you could try succulents or herbs (see p.116). The only limit is size: green wall plants need to be shallow-rooted, and should not naturally grow taller than 6–12 in (15–30 cm).

Color and contrast
Choose plants of varying textures, and at least one type that offers a pop of color.

How to create it

1

Check the wall is free of any cables. Position the structure level against the wall, then mark where screws will go. Drill into the wall at each marked location.

5

Select your most eye-catching or colorful plants and begin to position them evenly around the green wall. Gently firm them into position.

2

Hammer an anchor into each hole. Once all the required holes have been prepared, replace the structure and screw firmly into place.

3

If your structure is modular (as this one is), work up the wall one module at a time. Once the whole structure is mounted, check it is fully secure.

4

Fill each planting compartment with potting mix, along with a generous handful of fertilizer.

6

Working from the top down, fill the compartments with your remaining plants, tucking them in snugly together.

7

Water the entire green wall generously, ensuring that every compartment gets a thorough soaking around the plants' roots.

Get started with …
Plants for cracks and crevices

Gardens are full of awkward, small, strangely shaped gaps such as the base of
walls and steps. If weeds can grow there, something more desirable can, too,
and you can change the look of an area for the better. When choosing, check
whether the plants are sun- or shade-dwellers, and match them to your space.

1 **Mexican fleabane
(*Erigeron
karvinskianus*)**

☼ to 6in (15cm)

Seemingly in flower for
most of the year, this
little semi-evergreen
perennial bears masses
of daisylike flowers
that open pink and age
to white. It will make
you smile!

2 Hart's tongue fern (*Asplenium scolopendrium*)

☼ ☀ to 20 in (50 cm)

This evergreen fern has several cultivars with pretty fronds of varying shapes and sizes.

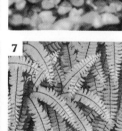

3 Houseleek (*Sempervivum*)

☼ to 4 in (10 cm)

Sempervivum species have lovely rosettes of succulent leaves that look almost cactus-like, forming little mounds and hummocks.

4 Sea thrift (*Armeria maritima*)

☼ to 8 in (20 cm)

An evergreen perennial, sea thrift forms cushions of green foliage with flowers like mini drumsticks.

5 Lady's mantle (*Alchemilla mollis*)

☼ to 8 in (20 cm)

A cottage garden favorite, lady's mantle has lime green flowers. Brush the seeds into narrow crevices and it will find its own way.

6 Mind-your-own-business (*Soleirolia soleirolii*)

☼ to 2 in (5 cm)

One of my favorites, mind-your-own-business is tolerant of some shade. Variegated and golden forms are available, too.

7 Common polypody (*Polypodium vulgare*)

☼ to 6 in (15 cm)

A cute little fern, this can sometimes be found growing on walls or rooftops.

8 *Euonymus fortunei* 'Kewensis'

☼ to 6 in (15 cm)

A lovely little evergreen shrub, this creeps and climbs and forms a dense mat of foliage.

Bulbs

Bulbs are a wonderfully convenient way of giving any garden or display of pots a color boost, without costing the earth. They are great to plant with children, and the anticipation of seeing them come into growth, and then flower, is always rewarding.

A bulb is like a condensed battery pack of life—a plant with leaves, stem, and flower, ready to go. Bulbs need little help to perform once planted, are affordable, and are often readily available—perfect for a rental gardener wanting a quick result. They generally come back year after year, so are also good for longer-term planting.

There are different types of bulb, flowering in spring, summer, or fall.

Simple display
A white variety of grape hyacinth (*Muscari*) is pretty in a group.

The basics

HOW TO PLANT A BULB

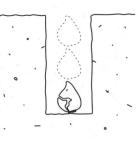

01
Dig a hole for the bulb. As a general rule of thumb, this should be two to three times the bulb's own depth. If planted too shallow, it may struggle in dry weather, or topple over when it flowers.

Spring-flowering bulbs include snowdrops, crocus, daffodils, tulips, and alliums, while lilies and gladioli flower in the summer; fall-flowering bulbs include colchicum (*Colchicum*) and nerines (see also pp.104–105).

Planting bulbs

Plant your chosen bulbs at the earliest opportunity after purchase, as they tend to be sold right around their ideal planting time. Most fall-planted bulbs flower from early spring into early summer. Spring is also a planting window for summer-flowering bulbs such as lilies and gladioli.

Generally, bulbs do not like to be in saturated ground, so avoid areas prone to waterlogging—though the odd winter puddle is fine. For a natural look in a border, scatter bulbs across the area, then follow with a trowel and plant them where they have landed (see below).

Naturalistic planting
Scatter bulbs across a bed and plant them where they fall for a naturally random positioning.

02
Place the bulb into the hole. Larger bulbs need to be planted the right way up, with the growing tip pointing upward and any roots facing down.

03
Fill the hole and continue to plant the rest of the bulbs, spacing them out according to packet recommendations. Keep well-watered, especially if the bulbs have been planted into containers.

Mixing bulbs with other plants
White daffodils (above) give height to this container display. In a mixed border (above right), tulips give a vivid block of color as well as striking form.

It's not always easy to tell which way is up when planting small bulbs such as crocus and scilla, but happily they can sort themselves out below ground. Larger, more expensive bulbs such as lilies are easier to assess and often have roots coming from their base.

Bulbs grow well in a pot. They are hungry and thirsty, so choose a good-quality potting mix and feed and water regularly as they grow.

Using bulbs in the garden

Bulbs such as crocus can cost just a few cents each, and tulips not a lot more, so if you plant them in a border, it is not a massive investment to leave behind. If you have gaps in a border, bulbs such as alliums and gladioli are great at "popping through" other plants and enlivening a space. With bulbs, more is definitely more—so be bold and adventurous. I have never heard a gardener confess to planting too many bulbs, and should you find yourself awash with flowers, they are great for a vase indoors!

If you have gaps in a border, bulbs such as alliums and gladioli are great at "popping through" other plants and enlivening a space.

Striking shapes
Globe-shaped allium flowers form a contrast
to the more delicate surrounding plants in
this large border. The smaller plants hide the
allium's leaves, and will come into their own as
the alliums dry out and lose their color.

Project
Layered bulb display

With a succession of bulbs in a single display, this project offers the best of spring in one pot and can be planted up quickly in the fall, before offering weeks of color into the spring.

You will need

- **A large plant pot, at least 2 ft (60 cm) deep,** with a drainage hole in the base
- **Slow-release fertilizer**
- **Potting mix**
- **A mixture of bulbs with different flowering times** (see pp.104-105) – you'll need 20-50 bulbs for each layer, depending on size of the bulbs and the size of your container
- **Decorative mulch,** such as wood chips or pine cones (optional)

The key to creating a layered bulb display is a generous pot, at least 2 ft (60 cm) deep, to provide enough room for both the potting mix and the multiple bulb layers. Because the bulb varieties used all emerge at different times, you end up with a display that offers successive flushes of color and interest from early February right through to May. This makes it ideal for gardeners who are short on space, as the one container will offer wave after wave of blooms. Spring bulbs need to be planted the fall before so, if need be, you can place the container somewhere discreet over winter, then move it to a more prominent spot once the first shoots start to peep through.

Because the display is so densely packed, it is unlikely to give such impressive results in the second year, so once the display is over, replant your bulbs in open ground if you have any available to you—or give them to a friend who has the space to set them free!

Late winter

Early spring

Mid-spring

Late spring

Creating the bulb layers

For this display, I created four layers of bulbs: snowdrops and dwarf irises, which flower in late winter (see p.101, top left); crocuses, which flower in early spring (top right); daffodils, which flower in mid-spring (bottom left); and tulips, which flower in late spring (bottom right). You can opt for whichever varieties you prefer, but try to use a shorter-growing daffodil variety if you can. The bulbs will generally be planted in reverse flowering order (so tulips first, then daffodils, and so on) as larger and later-flowering bulbs usually need greater depths. Always check the correct planting depths before you begin.

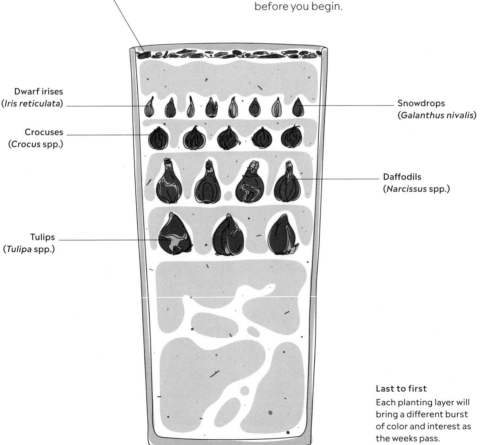

Mulch layer

Dwarf irises
(*Iris reticulata*)

Crocuses
(*Crocus* spp.)

Tulips
(*Tulipa* spp.)

Snowdrops
(*Galanthus nivalis*)

Daffodils
(*Narcissus* spp.)

Last to first
Each planting layer will bring a different burst of color and interest as the weeks pass.

How to create it

1  Fill the pot just over halfway with the potting mix. Add in a few generous pinches of fertilizer, then firm down the mix lightly—don't compact it too much.

2 Place the first layer of bulbs onto the potting mix, spacing them evenly. Cover with more potting mix and firm down lightly.

3  Repeat step 2 to create the next bulb layer. Continue until all the layers have been created, checking the correct planting depth for each bulb and making sure that each is planted accordingly.

4 Make sure to leave a gap between the surface of the potting mix and the lip of the pot—this will allow room for watering. Soak the potting mix thoroughly, until water flows from the bottom of the pot.

5  Cover the surface with decorative mulch, if desired. Water the pot regularly through winter and spring to prevent the potting mix from drying out, even before shoots start to appear.

Tidying up

As each layer finishes flowering and the next shoots start to appear, you can trim back the finished foliage so the next set of flowers is more visible.

Squirrel alert

If squirrels are frequent visitors to your yard, cover the pot with mesh over winter to stop them stealing your bulbs. Remove the mesh once shoots start to appear.

Get started with …
Bulbs

Bulbs and corms (which are similar and grown in the same way as bulbs) are wonderful little packages of color and excitement, ideal for both containers and open beds and borders. There are flowers for spring, summer, and fall. Many can live for years in good conditions, though they can also be treated like an annual and planted every year.

1 Daffodil 'Thalia' (*Narcissus* 'Thalia')

 12–18 in (30–45 cm)

This daffodil is a real favorite of mine—an elegant, clean white with several flower heads per stem in spring. It works well in both borders and pots.

2 Meadow saffron 'Waterlily'
(*Colchicum* 'Waterlily')

☀ ◐ 12 in (30 cm)

One of the most striking early fall flowers, this has double pink flowers. Other varieties are white or different shades of pink. The flowers appear after the leaves, which have died down by midsummer.

3 Snowdrop
(*Galanthus elwesii*)

☀ ◐ ☀ 4–6 in (10–15 cm)

This late winter flowering snowdrop has a good-size flower. It grows well in pots.

4 Tulip 'Queen of Night'

☀ 20–25 in (50–60 cm)

Striking, deep, dark flowers distinguish this spring tulip. It is a good height for pots and thrives in borders, too.

5 Grape hyacinth 'Peppermint'
(*Muscari armeniacum* 'Peppermint')

☀ ◐ 6–8 in (15–20 cm)

Inexpensive and easy to grow, this has unusual ice blue flowers in spring and can cope with poor soil.

6 *Allium* 'Purple Rain'

☀ to 24 in (60 cm)

An affordable bulb with impactful, tall flowers in early summer, this allium is also great for pollinators.

7 *Gladiolus*

☀ to 3 ft (1m)

Available in many different colors, gladiolus flowers in summer and is good for a sunny spot. It also makes a great cut flower. Plant the corms deep to help with stability when in flower.

8 Crocus
(*Crocus* 'Pickwick')

☀ ◐ to 8 in (20 cm)

An early-spring flowering corm, this can be grown through grass as well as in borders.

Growing your own

It's hugely satisfying to eat something that you've grown and harvested yourself, knowing that it's perfectly ripe, fresh, and homegrown. It's something everyone needs to try at least once—you really can taste the difference!

Some gardeners are completely committed to growing edible plants and will only grow herbs, fruit, and vegetables. In many cases, they can be just as beautiful as ornamental (nonedible) plants—and, of course, have the added bonus that they will end up on your dinner plate.

Raising crops while renting

You don't need huge beds to start growing your own edible crops. Many types of produce can succeed in relatively small spaces, including containers; just remember to check the plant's individual needs (see pp.114–117) before you start. If growing crops in pots, remember that they will need extra care to keep them well fed and watered (see pp.162–165).

Another challenge for those with small, urban spaces is adequate light. It's true that crops don't usually thrive in deep shade, but the likes of radishes, beets, and gooseberry plants will cope with dappled or light shade.

Most gardeners start with pots of herbs, or vegetables like lettuce and green beans that can be sown and harvested in the same year. Fruit trees may not be suitable for renters, especially if they plan to move in a year or two, but pot-grown fruit bushes may live for years if well cared for, offering harvest after harvest.

Choosing crops

Before you start, spend some time researching how long different edible crops take to grow. Some produce

Productive planting
Outdoor shelving provides an easy way to maximize growing space for these herbs, lettuces, and strawberries.

Containing crops
A raised bed (left) looks neat and attractive when full of rich soil and healthy crops. Vegetables such as lettuces and beans make a fresh, productive container display (below).

that is readily and cheaply available to buy in stores can take months to grow, so may not quite be worth the effort to grow yourself, whereas the likes of herbs and salad leaves can be picked within weeks, and taste far better when enjoyed fresh from the garden.

Think carefully about what produce you will actually want to eat, too. For example, I love Swiss chard sautéed in garlic and butter, so this homegrown crop would never go to waste. Swiss chard is an absolute joy to look at in the garden, too.

Be realistic

Becoming completely self-sufficient is a big task that needs a lot of space, skill, and planning, so don't expect to be eating platefuls of garden produce every day. Instead, view your crops as a supplement to your weekly shopping. The satisfaction of what you do harvest will exceed anything you buy, knowing you grew it!

Sturdy supports
Tomatoes flourish in the light on this balcony, but need to be tied to strong supports to help them stay upright in a potentially windy spot.

Becoming completely self-sufficient is a big task that needs a lot of space, skill, and planning, so don't expect to be eating platefuls of garden produce every day. View your crops as a supplement to your weekly shopping. The satisfaction of what you do harvest will exceed anything you buy!

Project
Raised vegetable bed

Because they are grown to be harvested, many
vegetables are short-lived and don't need deep
root runs in open ground. This means you can
grow them easily in mobile raised beds.

Mobile raised beds are effectively large
containers with legs. This allows them to be
positioned on hard surfaces, and when empty
of soil or plants, they can be repositioned or
even taken with you to your next home. With
them, you can chop and change what you grow,
and have several harvests from each season,
without needing to continually change the soil.
As they are larger than a typical container, they
also hold more soil, reducing the need for
regular watering. Usefully, their weight also
makes them stable.

Like any container, a mobile raised bed needs
drainage holes. Some are sold with ready-made
holes and plugs in the base; if so, remove the
plugs before planting. If your planter doesn't
come with drainage holes, you may need to
add a few yourself, using a drill (see p.82). This
project uses a selection of plug plants, which
are young plants bought directly from a garden
center or online nursery, ready to be planted
and grown on. Alternatively, you can transplant
seedlings you have raised yourself on a windowsill,
or even sow seed directly into the planter if the
conditions are suitable (see pp.52–55).

You will need

· A mobile planter or
  raised bed
· Potting mix
· Pelleted fertilizer
· Vegetable plants or
  plugs of your choice
· Labels (optional)

Potting mix costs

A top-quality potting mix is ideal for mobile raised beds. However, depending on the size of the container, it may be quite expensive to fill it up. If that's the case, try mixing in some partially composted bark chips, which tends to be a little cheaper. This often has a lower nutrient content and a poorer structure, but if it's enriched with organic pelleted fertilizer, it can help bulk out whatever potting mix you are able to afford.

Pest watch

Birds, insects, and other pests (see pp.170–171) may take a liking to your crops: carrot fly (which, as you might expect, attack carrots) and pigeons pecking at brassicas are among the most common challenges. That being said, you're unlikely to face too many pest problems if you're growing only a small number of crops on a balcony like the one shown here, but it pays to be vigilant.

Thirsty plants

Crops need moist (not waterlogged) soil to grow well, so remember to water them regularly. Avoid letting the soil dry out fully between waterings, as this can cause crops to develop defects.

How to create it

1

Assemble the planter, ensuring that the legs are secure. Position it in an easily accessible spot where it will receive plenty of sun throughout the day.

4

Working in rows, plant the plug plants and firm them gently into place. Planting in rows helps prevent vigorous plants from overtaking slower-growing ones—and it looks good, too.

2

If necessary, add drainage holes or remove any plugs (see p.110). Fill with potting mix to just below the rim, mixing in pelleted fertilizer as you go.

3

Carefully remove each young plug plant from its tray, taking care not to damage any delicate roots. Discard any weak or damaged plants.

5

Before planting larger plants, such as this chile pepper, lightly loosen the root ball with your fingers to encourage good growth. Don't overfill the planter: make sure everything has enough room to grow.

6

When the planter is full, water everything thoroughly, and continue to keep your crops well-watered as they grow (see opposite). Add labels if you think you may forget what you've planted where.

Get started with …
Homegrown crops

The range of edible plants is ever-evolving and improving. When choosing varieties, look for the All America Selections (AAS) winners, or read up on those that are most reliable. Remember, old heritage varieties are not always the best—sometimes there's a reason they fell out of favor! Weed regularly to help your crops thrive (see pp.178–181).

1 Radishes ☼

Quick-growing radishes are an easy starter crop, and taste great fresh from the garden.

- **Sow** between spring and fall, scattering the seeds in a thin row.
- **Thin out** (remove) weak seedlings to give the rest plenty of space to grow.
- **Harvest** when the radish is the size of a large cherry, and ideally eat that day. Don't leave them in the soil too long or they will turn woody.

2 Beets ☼

Easy to grow from seed, beets are really versatile in the kitchen. The roots come in colors from purple to orange, white, and striped, and young beet leaves are also edible.

- **Sow** thinly from late spring onward, in the place where they are to mature—they ideally don't like to be transplanted.
- **Harvest** at intervals along the row to allow others space to grow larger. Don't let them grow too large or they will turn woody—golf-ball size is good.

3 Zucchini ☼

A zucchini plant grows quite large, but crops until fall if kept fed and watered, so is excellent value.

- **Sow** indoors in early spring, preferably at a temperature of about 68°F (20°C).
- **Harden off** and then plant out in late spring after frosts.
- **Harvest** young fruits often for best flavor and to encourage more to develop.

4 Tomatoes ☼

The sunnier the space, the happier tomatoes will be. Basket and container varieties are available, and all tomatoes need regular food and water.

- **Sow** indoors in early spring.
- **Plant outside** when all risk of frost is over. Feed and water well.
- **Harvest** individual tomatoes when ripe.

5 Lettuce ☼

Attractive to look at, versatile, and easy to grow, lettuce is always best served fresh from the garden (or balcony).

- **Sow** direct in the ground or in a pot in late spring, a few seeds at a time.
- **Water well.**
- **Harvest** loose-leaf lettuces whole or pick individual leaves. For lettuces that form heads, cut them off whole at the stalk.

6 Herbs ☼

Chives, mint, thyme, oregano, and rosemary are all easy to grow and can be long-lived. They are often best bought as potted plants and planted out. Parsley, basil, and cilantro are shorter-lived, so are usually replaced every spring.

- **Sow** in warm soil in spring. Plant hardy, pot-grown herbs at any time of year.
- **Water** regularly.
- **Pick regularly** once established to encourage new leaves.

7 Bush green beans
☼

Compact, heavy cropping, and delicious when fresh, bush green beans are easy to grow and give a good yield for the comparatively small space they inhabit. They like a warm, wind-free spot.

- **Sow** indoors in mid-spring, or outside in late spring after the frosts.
- **Water often** so the soil remains moist

and the plants can grow steadily.

- **Use** small pea sticks (twiggy supports) to stop plants laden with beans from toppling over.
- **Harvest** after two or three months. Pick the beans every few days when they are young and slender for the best taste.

8 Swiss chard ☀

Colorful and delicious, chard continues into the winter months. It can be harvested whenever it's required in the kitchen. Young leaves are eaten whole in salads, and fully grown leaves are often separated into stem and leaf for cooking.

- **Sow** in spring for crops until the fall, then sow again in summer for crops the following spring.
- **Water regularly.**
- **Harvest** leaves individually. They can be cut when very young or fully grown.

9 Strawberries ☀

A versatile fruit plant, strawberries have been bred to create many varieties, including ones with attractive pink flowers and others more suited to pots and hanging baskets.

- **Plant** pot-grown strawberries out in spring and leave them to establish.
- **Water regularly** when newly planted and when berries are developing. Leave plants in pots or the ground to crop year after year, tidying up old leaves in spring. Protect from birds with netting if necessary.
- **Harvest** when ripe and eat as soon as possible! Crops are likely to be light in the first year of planting.

10 Blueberries ☀

Able to live successfully in pots for many years, blueberry plants enjoy sun and some shade and produce lovely spring flowers and striking fall color. The fruit is delicious freshly picked, and may save you some money as it's relatively expensive to buy.

- **Plant** in winter if possible. Blueberries grow naturally in acidic soil, but still flourish in a neutral soil, and will live happily in containers, in acidic potting mix.
- **Prune** out old, diseased, or damaged stems in winter once the bush is mature.
- **Pick** individual berries when they are plump and slightly soft.

Making it your own

You can justify putting even more time and effort into your yard if you have a long lease. When you can start to really think ahead in years instead of months, new gardening opportunities open up, not least in the form of perennials or even trees, which will grow and mature throughout your tenancy.

Growing perennials

Quick-growing perennials are excellent value for money, especially for renters who plan to stay put for a long time. As their name suggests, they are long-lasting, living and growing for many years, and can often provide a great display throughout much of the growing season each year.

The opposite of annuals (see pp.42–45), perennials come back every year, usually returning in the spring after a dormant winter. They are a staple of many cottage gardens, herbaceous borders, and mass plantings. Many are also great for pollinating insects, and can give a balanced and structured look to a garden space. Shrubs are essentially perennial plants with woody stems. They provide height and structure to a border, along with a good show of flowers each year.

Planting perennials

Perennials should ideally be planted in either spring or fall. Keep spring plantings well-watered during their first summer, so they don't dry out before they establish themselves.

Perennials can "bulk up" very quickly, giving you a rewarding display in a short space of time, so remember to allow room between plants when you prepare your border (see also p.55). They can also grow quite tall and may require support to stop them toppling over if they have spindly stems, top-heavy flowers, or if they grow taller than 3 ft (1m). To do this, insert sturdy twigs, sticks, or a bamboo cane into the plant, right beside the crown (where the stems emerge from the roots), and tie in with string if necessary. This is best done in the winter months, for the plant to then grow through them in the summer months.

Pruning perennials

Deciduous perennials need to be cut back to ground level in late winter. This encourages new stems to emerge in spring, keeps the plant a manageable size, and prevents it from becoming overwhelmed by unproductive stems from the previous year. Check the plant's individual needs before pruning.

Perennials are a staple of many cottage gardens, herbaceous borders, and mass plantings. Many are also great for pollinating insects, and can give a balanced and structured look to a garden space.

Perennial mixture
Packed with a combination of herbaceous perennials, this bed provides varied color, form, and texture through the growing season.

Herbaceous border
These perennials are mixed in
with evergreen grasses. The
perennials are at their best in
summer, and fade in the fall.

Moving on

Perennial borders are a great investment if you're planning to stay in one place for a long time, but what if you do need to move? Most perennials and smaller shrubs can be transplanted into containers for the trip—just make sure that the pot is large enough to comfortably fit the root ball.

Alternatively, you can take just part of an established perennial with you to grow on yourself. To do this, lift the plant and carefully slice away a piece by cutting into the crown with a sharp spade, making sure that the newly divided piece has a good piece of root on it. Plant this new cutting into a small pot of fresh potting mix to take with you, cutting it back by half to reduce stress to the plant from transplanting, then replace the plant back into its original position. The division will grow and become a part of your next garden, while the established plant you leave behind can be inherited and cared for by future tenants.

Playing with height
Perennials can be the centerpiece of a garden planting, giving height within a space (top left). Alternatively, lower-growing perennials can form more of an edging feature (left).

Project
Summer perennial border

With a profusion of flower color, a perennial border offers a long season of interest and will perform year on year. Low maintenance and high impact, perennials are garden favorites.

While perennials return year after year, as their name suggests, that doesn't always mean that they will flower for long periods of time each year. The secret to a good perennial border is to include a mix of different species that flower at different times throughout the summer months, so you can guarantee blooms during the time of year that you're most likely to be spending time in your garden.

The temptation can be to buy many different types of perennial so you have constant flowering, but having such a varied assortment rarely works well visually, especially in a small space. I recommend no more than three to five varieties for a small border (or five to seven for larger spaces), repeating one or two types through the border to help weave it all together.

You will need

· Well-rotted manure
· A garden fork
· Selection of
  perennial plants
· A spade for planting
· Pelleted manure
· Ornamental mulch,
  such as a shredded
  bark (optional)

How to create it

1 Clear the bed of weeds and debris. Using a fork to incorporate, enrich with well-rotted manure, then lightly tread to remove air pockets.

2 Arrange the plants on the bed, still in their pots, to figure out your planting plan (see below). Move them around until you are happy with their locations.

3 Working from one end of the bed to the other, plant the perennials, loosening their root balls before firming them into the soil.

Designing your border

When planning what to plant where, it's important to give each plant the space it will need as it matures. Consider the heights of plants, colors, and leaf texture as you visualize how your border will look. In this border, I opted for rose 'Blue Eyes', Bowman's root (*Gillenia trifoliata*), and bellflower (*Campanula* 'Loddon Anna'). You can also plant bulbs into the border among the perennials (see pp.96–99).

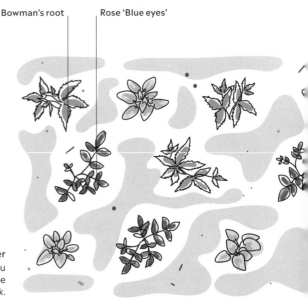

Bowman's root   Rose 'Blue eyes'

Visualizing your border
A simple sketch helps you check spacing and imagine how your border will look.

4

Scatter pelleted manure around the plants, taking care to avoid the crowns. Cover with an ornamental mulch if you wish. Water the bed well.

Caring for your young plants

Water the bed after planting to activate the manure pellets and settle the plants into their new position. Continue to water during dry periods in the first summer. As young perennials grow, they can end up toppling over. Use bamboo canes or sticks to support them as they mature.

Small start

If you can, buy perennials in 3½in (9 cm) or 1¾ pint (1 liter) pots in the winter or early spring. They may only look like a few small shoots, but they are cheaper than the same plants bought in flower over summer—and will grow just as well.

Best value
Small perennials are cheaper to buy than larger ones, and will soon grow to form good-size plants.

Bellflower
'Loddon Anna'

Get started with …
Perennials

Herbaceous perennials are plants that flower, die down, and then return year after year. This much-treasured group of plants has a wide spectrum of flowering times, and some even flower in the depths of winter. Many perennials increase their root systems as they get older, creating bigger and bolder displays. Those featured here flower in summer.

1 *Geum* 'Totally Tangerine'

☼ ☀ 24–36in (60–90 cm)

This deciduous perennial produces cheerful orange flowers from early summer onward. While it can grow tall enough to provide structure to a border, it doesn't need staking.

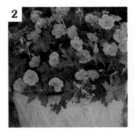

2 *Geranium* 'Rozanne'

☼ ☀ 12–36in (30–90 cm)

Brilliant for billowing over bed edges and scrambling through plants, this geranium flowers all summer.

3 Peruvian lily (*Alstroemeria* 'Indian Summer')

☼ ☀ to 3ft (1m)

The Peruvian lily's dark foliage contrasts wonderfully with warm, rich orange and red summer flowers.

**4 Plantain lily
(*Hosta* 'Halcyon')**
☼ ☀ to 24 in (60 cm)

A striking blue-leaved perennial, this hosta is happy in part sun or shade. It has showy pink flowers in early summer.

**5 Culver's root
(*Veronicastrum
virginicum* 'Fascination')**
☼ to 5 ft (1.5 m)

Wonderful for bees, this tall perennial is perfect for the back of the border, flowering in mid- to late summer.

**6 White gaura
(*Oenothera
lindheimeri*)**
☼ to 4 ft (1.2 m)

Light, airy, butterfly-like white flowers flutter over a border in early to midsummer.

**7 Yellow daylily
(*Hemerocallis
lilioasphodelus*)**
☼ ☼ to 3 ft (1 m)

This daylily produces an abundance of yellow flowers in early to midsummer. Does not need staking.

**8 Red hot poker
(*Kniphofia* 'Tawny King')**
☼ to 3 ft (1 m)

The tall, two-toned mid- to late summer flowering spikes of this red hot poker are a striking addition to any garden.

Planting a tree

While a tree might not seem like an option when you're
renting, it's worth considering if you have the space.
Not only will a tree look great in your yard, but it
is also one of the kindest things you can do for the
planet—and all for the price of carryout for two.

Trees are available at most garden centers and nurseries, or online from plant suppliers. Container-grown trees are the most readily available and convenient to buy, and can be planted at any time of the year. If your budget is limited, buy smaller; for example, some trees are available in a 7.5 liter pot. Deciduous trees are often cheaper than evergreen trees, and slow-growing evergreens tend to be the most expensive of all.

In many cases, younger trees grow more quickly than semi-mature trees bought in at a larger size, simply because older trees take longer to settle in—though older trees have the bonus of delivering instant impact. In some situations (often in urban areas), gardeners may plant varieties that grow too tall or too vigorously in restricted spaces. Over time, they become a serious problem, either by obstructing light or by causing structural damage to walls and foundations with their growing roots. The problem in this case isn't the tree, it's the gardener: they haven't chosen the right species to suit their space. For this reason, it's best to avoid vigorous species such as poplar (*Populus*), willow (*Salix*), and gum (*Eucalyptus*). Make sure to check the label on the tree before buying to see its dimensions when fully grown.

Planting into a container

Trees are always happiest in the ground, but if your landlord will not agree to one (or if your outdoor space is totally paved over) consider using a container instead (see pp.134–137). Pot-grown trees require more care than ground-planted ones, as they need to be kept well fed and watered, but they will flourish for several years. They can also be taken with you when you move, and planted out at a later opportunity (see p.133).

A potted fig tree
Figs are very vigorous, and a pot restricts their size. In its large, shiny pot, this fig makes an exotic statement.

Trees with impact
This container group (above) offers
evergreen foliage. Clipped hornbeams
(right) enhance a tight space.

Tree planting basics

The best time to plant a tree in the
ground is fall or spring. Choose a
clear space with plenty of good
light and air circulation, and
remember to look up and assess the
headroom space, too. It sounds
obvious, but all too often trees are
planted in the shade of other trees,
or in a position directly alongside a
large building, which only results in
lopsided growth.

Supporting young trees

If a newly planted tree is at risk of
being rocked back and forth by the
wind, it usually needs staking for the
first 12–18 months. Insert a stake into
the ground at the base of the tree

at a 45-degree angle, placing it on
the side of the tree stem where the
prevailing wind hits it—you want the
tree to blow away from the stake, not
into it. Secure to the tree with a tie.

KEEP YOUR *landlord* IN THE LOOP

Landlords may be disinclined to have a tree in
their yard, given that some could affect house
foundations. Reassure them by doing your homework
before speaking to them. If you suggest only slow-
growing varieties that will remain compact when fully
grown, that will most likely inspire their confidence.

The basics
HOW TO PLANT A TREE

01
While the tree is still in its container, thoroughly soak the root ball. In the meantime, measure the container, then dig a hole just as deep and up to three times as wide if the soil is poor.

02
Remove the tree from the pot and lightly tease out the roots. Place the tree in the center of the hole, making sure that the root flare (the point where the roots emerge from the stem) sits slightly above ground level.

03
Back-fill the hole with the soil you dug out, and firm gently with your foot. Stake the tree if necessary (see opposite). Add a doughnut of mulch at the base, ensuring it doesn't touch the stem.

04
Water the newly planted tree thoroughly, so the roots are properly drenched. Continue to water in dry spells during the first summer season after planting.

Project
Tree in a pot

For rental gardeners without access to ground, or those who may not wish to commit a tree to a yard where they aren't planning to stay for long, a pot-planted tree is ideal.

You will need

- **A heavy pot,** large enough to contain the root ball easily
- **A slow-growing tree** (see pp.138–139)
- **Enriched potting mix**
- **Slow-release fertilizer**
- **A stake or bamboo cane** (depending on the tree)
- **Garden twine**
- **3–5 plants** for the underplanting
- **Mulch** (optional)

While trees are best planted in the ground (see pp.132–133), a young tree in a large pot has the potential to last for many years if fed and watered correctly, and can brighten up even a small, paved-over outdoor space. As a bonus, you can take a potted tree with you, and if and when you do find yourself with your own yard, you can plant the tree in the ground.

People are often surprised to learn that a tree can live in a pot. It's true that some aren't suited to the task: quick-growing, thirsty trees such as birch (*Betula*), gum (*Eucalyptus*), and willow (*Salix*) will quickly become root-bound if planted into a container, exhausting the soil and becoming top-heavy. Instead, opt for trees such as strawberry tree (*Arbutus unedo*), star magnolia (*Magnolia stellata*), or paperback maple (*Acer griseum*); here, I have used a Chilean myrtle (*Luma apiculata*).

To give the tree an added burst of color, underplant it with low or trailing plants. If the base is in shade, choose ferns or woodland plants like *Polypodium* or *Pachysandra*; if in sun, use alpines, succulents, or even Mediterranean herbs such as trailing rosemary or sage.

Providing support

If the tree appears to wobble in its pot, use a stake or cane to add support, inserting it alongside the tree stem. Never be tempted to plant the tree deeper; the root flare must always be visible (see p.133) for the tree to survive. Always make sure a potted tree is well watered before windy weather is forecast, as the extra moisture will help increase weight, thus stabilizing it.

Repotting and caring for your tree

Your tree will be happy for 3–5 years in the same pot if fed and watered regularly during the growing season (between April and October). Every couple of years, the tree can be slid out of its pot for repotting. Using a wood saw or an old bread knife, saw off the bottom 20 percent of the root ball, and place fresh potting mix in the bottom of the pot, with added slow-release fertilizer. Place the tree back into the same pot. This new rooting space will aid good health and help keep the tree looking its best.

Preparing the root ball
Use a hand fork to lightly tease out any congested roots before replanting the tree.

How to create it

1

Place the pot in its final position. Measure the root ball's depth, then fill the pot with enough potting mix to allow the root flare to sit at the correct final level (see p.133).

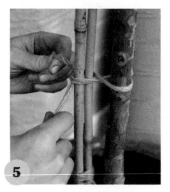

5

If the tree is very tall, wobbly, or positioned in a windy site, insert a stake carefully into the pot. Secure it to the trunk with string, using figure-eight knots as shown.

2 Remove the tree from its plastic pot, then gently tease out any congested roots. Carefully lift it into the decorative pot.

3 Pack fresh potting mix around the root ball, ensuring that the root flare is visible. Support the main stem to ensure that the tree stays upright.

4 Leave around 2 in (5 cm) of space between the potting mix and the pot rim. Work a slow-release fertilizer into the top 4 in (10 cm).

6 Underplant the tree with your chosen plants, spacing them around the base of the tree evenly. Do not worry if they slightly intrude into the tree's root ball.

7 Add a layer of decorative mulch to the top of the potting mix, if desired. Water the pot well so the soil is thoroughly moist and excess can be seen draining from the base.

Get started with …
Trees

Bringing a sense of structure and permanence to a place, trees are valuable aesthetically, and great for both wildlife and carbon absorption. There is a tree for just about every situation, and many will live happily in pots until the opportunity comes around to plant them into the ground. The trees here will all grow in a container; the heights given are after about 10 years of growth.

**1 Strawberry tree
(*Arbutus unedo* 'Rubra')**
☼ ☼ 6½ ft (2 m)

It's hard to go wrong with this slow-growing evergreen. It offers bell-like pink flowers in late summer and orange fruits that ripen to red through the fall months.

**2 *Acer campestre*
'Evenley Red'**
☼ ☼ 13 ft (4 m)

Tolerant of the coldest of winter conditions, this maple tree is known for its great fall leaf color.

**3 *Aesculus* x *neglecta*
'Autumn Fire'**
☼ 10 ft (3 m)

This deciduous tree has eye-catching new spring leaves, beautiful summer flowers, and vibrant fall color.

4 *Koelreuteria paniculata* **'Coral Sun'**

☀ ☀ 13 ft (4 m)

In my opinion this tree deserves more attention. The vibrant young leaves in spring are spectacular, and are followed by summer flowers that go on to produce golden, highly unusual seed capsules.

5 *Amelanchier* x *grandiflora* **'Ballerina'**

☀ ☀ 10 ft (3 m)

In spring, this deciduous tree's coppery young leaves are complemented by dainty white flowers.

6 *Magnolia grandiflora* **'Kay Parris'**

☀ 10 ft (3 m)

This evergreen magnolia has dainty leaves with rusty brown undersides and lemon meringue pie–scented, cream flowers in summer.

7 *Malus* **'Indian Magic'**

☀ 13 ft (4 m)

The spring blossom of this ornamental crab apple is strikingly large. Come fall, birds will love the tree's pretty red fruits.

8 *Prunus* **'The Bride'**

☀ 13 ft (4 m)

All the magic of cherry blossom in a modest-size tree, with elegant white spring flowers and good fall leaf color.

Working with water

Even the smallest of water features can introduce a
tranquility to your space that little else can match.
A mini-pond stocked with a few aquatic plants will
encourage wildlife, while the soothing trickle of
running water can mask less desirable sounds.

Ponds and water features offer many
benefits to wildlife (see pp.172–175),
but digging a pond isn't an option
open to everyone. Possible issues
can include a lack of space or open
ground, concerns for young children
playing near open water, and—for
renters—potential pushback from
landlords. For all of these issues,
however, there is an alternative: using
watertight containers.

Mini-ponds

Life does not exist without water, and
the smallest dish of standing water will
be used by insects and birds within a
surprisingly short space of time. My
neighbor's cat often visits my yard to
drink from my water feature—despite
having a fresher water supply on the
other side of the fence!

A container pond can become a
real feature, especially if it contains a
water lily or other water plant (see
pp.148–149) or a simple, small bubble
fountain jet to bring the sound of
water to the space.

Do not add goldfish to a mini-pond.
Their waste will raise the nutrient
content of the water, increasing the
likelihood of algae (see pp.148–149).
Life in a relatively small pot is not
great for the welfare of the fish,
either. They are also at risk of freezing
solid in the winter, and are easy prey
for local wildlife.

For an eye-catching and multisensory water feature, you need to add
movement. Nothing quite beats the soothing sound of flowing water—and
it's bound to make an impressive centerpiece, too.

Pebble fountain
You don't need a large
space to introduce the
magic of water.

Water features

For a multisensory water feature, you need to add movement. Nothing quite beats the soothing sound of flowing water, while the sight of it is bound to make an impressive centerpiece.

Creating a pond with flowing water is easier than you might think. You don't need to connect the feature up to the faucet or build a permanent installation. In my garden, I have built a water feature within a large container, with a pump and a decorative mask. The pump draws water up through a length of hose and out through a spout positioned behind the mouth of the mask, creating a low, bubbling jet of water that flows through the mask and back into the container.

Many styles of self-contained water feature are available. Some of these are solar-powered, so require no outdoor electrical outlets and are easy to set up because the water simply circulates in a loop cycle.

While this sort of water feature won't encourage wildlife in the same way as a mini-pond, it will still provide water for birds to bathe in, while the movement will help reduce algae buildup. Make sure you buy a pump that is strong enough to move the water effectively; the manufacturer's guidelines will explain the volume of water the pump is suitable for.

Don't leave the water feature on all the time: aside from wasting energy, the water level will soon deplete, especially if it splashes a lot. The pump can even be damaged beyond repair if left to run completely dry. Instead, turn the feature on while you are there to enjoy the sight and sound of it.

Using stone
An old stone trough (left) makes a tranquil pool. A simple orb (above) overflows into a dish.

Water spout
In my own garden, a spouting mask creates a surprising amount of watery noise, drowning out the sound of all my neighbors!

Life does not exist without water, and the smallest dish of standing water will be used by insects and birds within a surprisingly short space of time. In my garden, my neighbor's cat visits to drink from my water feature, despite having a fresher water supply on the other side of the fence!

Project
Water lily container pond

While renters may not be able to dig a full-size
pond, a container provides all of the pleasures
of one in miniature: a calming sight dotted with
flowers, and plenty of water for wildlife to drink.

Any watertight container can be turned into a
mini-pond: a half-barrel, old sink, or even a large
plant pot, provided that it does not have a
drainage hole. DIY stores and garden centers
should stock something suitable, or for a
cheaper, more sustainable option, check out
salvage yards or your local Freecycle site.

While you can use any pond plant for this
project, as long as you can offer the correct
planting depth for its roots (see pp.148–149), a
single water lily will give your pond that added
wow factor, especially as they flower all summer.
Whatever you plant, use aquatic potting mix
instead of multipurpose, as it is better at
supporting aquatic plants longer term and
holding their structure under water. Aquatic
mix is heavier than others, resulting in less
displacement when you pour in the water.

The biggest challenge in a mini-pond is algae,
which develops on the surface of warm water
that has a high nutrient content. It looks
unsightly and smothers your pond plants
by blocking light to them. Fortunately, there
are several ways to prevent or reduce algal
growth (see p.146).

You will need

- **Large container,** at least
  18 in (45 cm) deep
- **Aquatic potting mix**
- **Grit**
- **Dwarf water lily**
  (see p.148)
- **Small container**
- **Watering can** or hose

Dealing with algae

Warm water encourages algae, so to prevent it building up too quickly, you need to take steps to keep the water relatively cool. For example, small container ponds warm up faster than larger ones, so opt for the biggest container you can. Likewise, avoid positioning the pond in full sun. While some warmth is needed, putting your pond in a spot that gets full midday sun will heat it up too much. A semi-shaded area that gets some morning or late afternoon sun is best.

If possible, use rainwater to fill your pond, as this contains fewer nutrients than tap water. Adding at least one aquatic plant will also help reduce algae levels, as it will happily make use of the nutrients the algae would take.

If algae does appear on the surface, simply poke in a bamboo cane and twist. This will wrap the algae into a satisfying lump on the end of the cane, which can then be slid off into the compost pile or popped into the back of the border to break down.

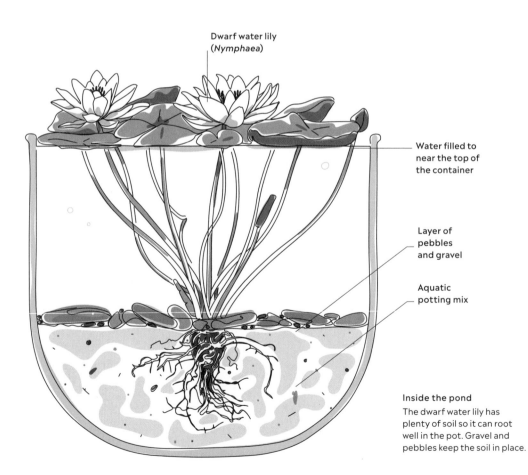

Dwarf water lily
(*Nymphaea*)

Water filled to
near the top of
the container

Layer of
pebbles
and gravel

Aquatic
potting mix

Inside the pond
The dwarf water lily has plenty of soil so it can root well in the pot. Gravel and pebbles keep the soil in place.

How to create it

1 Position the container in a spot that gets some sunlight (but ideally not full midday sun, see opposite). Make sure that the container is level and watertight.

2 Fill the pot about one-quarter full with aquatic potting mix. Make a well in the center large enough to hold the water lily's root ball.

3 Plant the water lily, firming it into place. Press down the surface of the soil until smooth and level.

4 Weigh down the soil with a thick layer of pebbles and gravel, until the surface is completely covered. Place a small container on the surface of the gravel.

5 With a watering can or hose, pour water into the small container. This will overflow and begin to fill the pond without dislodging the gravel layer or soil beneath.

6 Remove the container when it is completely submerged by water. Continue filling the pond gently. If anything is dislodged and the water becomes cloudy, give it a few hours and it should settle and clear.

Get started with …
Water plants

Water brings both wildlife and tranquility to a space. Since it's unlikely that you will be digging a pond in a rental yard, the aquatic options here all suit the conditions of a container pond (see pp.144–147). Their ornamental beauty is best appreciated close up, too.

1 Dwarf water lily (*Nymphaea* spp.)
☼ ☽ Growth speed: slow

Sometimes listed as Pygmaea types, dwarf or miniature water lilies are a slightly smaller form of the classic water lily. Recommended cultivars include 'Aurora' and 'Indiana'. Planting depth 12–16 in (30–40 cm).

2 Water hawthorn (*Aponogeton distachyos*)

☀ ◐ Growth speed: medium

This pond plant has floating leaves and unusual-looking white flowers. Planting depth 12–16 in (30–40 cm).

3 Japanese water iris (*Iris ensata*)

☀ ◐ Growth speed: slow

This wonderful iris is available in whites, purples, and yellows. It needs to be planted very shallowly, in less than 2 in (5 cm) of water; for deeper containers, position the iris (in a planting basket) on a stack of bricks to reach the correct height.

4 Pickerel weed (*Pontederia cordata*)

☀ ◐ Growth speed: fast

This is a reliable and vigorous plant, with bluish-purple flowers in late summer and attractive foliage. Plant at a depth of 2–6 in (5–15 cm).

5 Miniature cattail (*Typha minima*)

☀ ◐ Growth speed: medium

A miniature species of the classic reed, the grasslike foliage and mini seed heads of this plant are a real attraction. Planting depth 4–6 in (10–15 cm).

All about lawns

There's nothing better than kicking back or enjoying a picnic in the summer on lush, green grass. If you're lucky enough to have a lawn, it pays to take care of it well. And if you don't, creating your own may be easier than you think.

Lawn refresh
No one wants a patchy or semi-bald lawn. Neaten edges around borders with a half-moon edger, and fix bald patches by raking them free of debris, scattering over fresh grass, and watering well.

For many people, a traditional yard means a perfect lawn surrounded by borders of plants, with a tree in a corner. That vision may be far from the reality for many rental gardeners, but that doesn't mean that you can't make the most of whatever grass your outdoor space may offer.

Essential lawn care

It pays to take care of any lawn that your rental property may have. Unless you have a grass-free lawn of small, creeping plants (see pp.154–157), you're going to need a lawnmower.

A lawn is best mowed regularly in the summer, typically weekly if it is actively growing; leaving it to become long and then cutting it short will not give the best results. If you don't use your lawn very much, you can choose

to leave it unmown in early summer for 1–2 months. This allows a chance for any flowering plants naturally present within the lawn to bloom, supporting local biodiversity.

Keep edges trimmed, particularly near borders and paths (see above). If the lawn turns brown in hot summer weather, don't worry too much—it will quickly recover (see p.164).

Creating a new lawn

If you have a patch of open soil, why not establish your own lawn? There are two methods you can try.

KEEP YOUR *landlord* IN THE LOOP

Your lease should spell out if the lawn is your responsibility or the landlord's. If yours, see if your landlord will provide a lawnmower.

Green, green grass
While grass lawns need to be mowed, they are far better than any plastic alternative.

Grass seed offers a relatively cheap option, although the downside is that it takes a few months to see results. You can buy a variety of different grass seed mixes, each designed to suit your particular needs, such as those that are tailored for shady spaces.

You can seed an entire lawn if you wish; or, if you've inherited an existing lawn dotted with bald patches, you can freshen it up using grass seed.

With a rake, fluff up the top soil of the sparse area, then scatter a handful of seed and water well.

If you want really quick results, sod (mats of pre-grown grass) is the way to go. While more expensive, it will instantly transform your space into a lush, green yard. It is best laid the in the fall. Sod needs a lot of water during dry weather—don't plan a vacation directly after laying it!

Longer lawn
Leaving the grass longer can benefit wildlife, and looks good in an informal setting. It can be helpful to trim the edges from time to time to keep plants and grass separate.

In recent years, plastic grass has become very popular for creating an instant "lawn" that seemingly needs no maintenance. Resist the temptation. Plastic grass is terrible for the environment.

Clean lines
The rectangular lawn complements the geometric lines of this house for a stylish and easy-to-maintain yard.

Plastic isn't the answer

In recent years, plastic grass has become very popular for creating an instant "lawn" that seemingly needs no maintenance. Resist the temptation. Plastic grass is terrible for the environment. It prevents real plants from growing in the space, leaving fewer opportunities for pollinators and other vital insects to live and feed, and plastic grass is also a single-use plastic that will, before too long, end up in a landfill.

It isn't great for the gardener, either. In hot weather the plastic heats up, and does not provide the cool cushion of a real lawn. Over time, it wears out, and accumulates dust and debris that allows moss and weeds to grow.

Lawn edges
Having paving right up to the lawn edges gives a neat appearance and makes the lawn easier to mow.

Project
Grass-free lawn

If you want to add a patch of greenery to your yard but aren't able to mow and maintain it, a grass-free lawn is a colorful, environmentally beneficial alternative to hard landscaping.

Grass-free lawns are becoming increasingly popular, with many seeing them as a more eco-friendly alternative to traditional lawns, which often require more water and energy (from mowing) in order to keep them green and pristine.

This project is made up of a selection of low-growing plants (see pp.158–159), which can be bought as plugs (young plants) or in larger pots that can be split apart. Once planted, they naturally spread to create a diverse and multicolored patchwork that will support a wide variety of wildlife over time. Spring is the best time to complete this project, as that is when the plants begin active growth.

If you are starting with smaller plants, don't expect a finished effect on day one; however, by their nature these plants spread quickly, and you should soon see results. This type of grass-free lawn can be trodden on occasionally, but will not take regular foot traffic.

You will need

- Rake
- Spade
- Low-growing plants (see pp.158–159), either as larger plants or as plugs
- Hand trowel
- Hose with spray nozzle or watering can with rose

Laying sedum matting

Another way of achieving a grass-free lawn is to use sedum matting. While you won't achieve the same unique patchwork effect, it will give you an almost instant result. To lay sedum matting, prepare the ground as you would for plug plants (see steps 1–2), ideally in an area that gets full sun. Roll out the matting and cut to fit the space as needed. To prevent birds from pulling the matting up, pin it down around the edges with U-shaped hooks; these are available online or in garden centers, or you can make them from old wire coat hangers. Water in well.

Caring for grass-free lawns

The lawn will need watering for its first summer if there is little rain. Allow a few weeks after planting before walking on your lawn. If you want to keep the lawn low and bushy, cut with shears or a lawnmower periodically in summer to stop the plants producing flowers, which can grow tall.

Shades of green
Lysimachia, Fragaria, Prunella, Leptinella, and *Sagina* spread and knit together to create a tapestry-like effect.

How to create it

1

Clear all vegetation from the area in which you want to create your grass-free lawn. Loosen the top layer with a fork and rake it as level as you can.

4

If you have bought larger plants, divide each one into 2–3 pieces, making sure that each piece remains attached to a chunk of roots.

2

If the area is uneven, level it out by moving spadefuls of soil into any hollow areas. Tread across the whole area with small steps to remove any air bubbles.

3

Arrange the plants in their pots across the area, spacing them out slightly. Group the varieties in free-form shapes for best effect, as shown.

5

Plant the lawn-alternative plants, digging a small hole and firming each one into place. Make sure to distribute them evenly across the area.

6

Water the planted area carefully, using a hose with a fine spray nozzle (or a watering can with a rose, if the area is small) to avoid washing away soil from around the roots.

Get started with …
Lawn-alternative plants

You don't always need grass to create a green space. These low-growing, mat-forming plants are loved by pollinators and can be combined into an eye-catching patchwork (see pp.154–157) if use of the space is light—they won't take as much wear as a regular lawn. Speak to your landlord before starting your alternative lawn, as these plants can naturally spread over time.

1 **Creeping thyme (*Thymus serpyllum*)**

☼ 4 in (10 cm)

Also known as wild thyme, this plant is a close relative of the culinary herb. It has the same scent that you will recognize from the kitchen and, if left to flower, the pale pink blooms are great for bees, too.

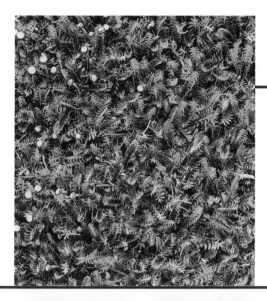

2 Leptinella (*Leptinella squalida*)
☼ 4 in (10 cm)

This beautiful, fernlike creeping plant from New Zealand grows best on lighter soils. It has flowers like small buttons.

3 Clover (*Trifolium repens*)
☼ 4 in (10 cm)

While some consider clover to be a weed, it is a great lawn alternative. Loved by bees, it is available in a range of different colors.

4 Chamomile (*Chamaemelum nobile*)
☼ 4 in (10 cm)

Chamomile offers scented foliage. It grows best in sunny areas that are neither too dry nor too wet.

5 Corsican mint (*Mentha requienii*)
☼ 4 in (10 cm)

Corsican mint develops into a tough, evergreen carpet over time, and releases a minty aroma when disturbed.

6 Creeping Jenny (*Lysimachia nummularia*)
☼ ☼ 4 in (10 cm)

Available in both green and golden forms, this is a great choice for poorly drained sites.

7 Sedum
☼ 4 in (10 cm)

Wonderful for sunny sites with well drained, often poor soils, sedum only tolerate light use.

8 Moss
☼ 4 in (10 cm)

It might sound strange, but if your lawn already contains more moss than anything else—especially in a shady area—why not embrace it? Simply remove any other plants from the lawn and let the moss thrive.

Taking care of your space

As well as tending to the plants
you already have and those you
have planted yourself, it pays to
keep your outdoor space up to
scratch by minimizing weeds and
maintaining any hard surfaces.
Taking care of a yard is also about
caring for the wildlife that visits
it, and in this chapter you'll find
ideas to achieve just that.

Watering and feeding

Understanding when and how to water and feed your plants is key to keeping your outdoor space looking great and getting the best out of your plants and crops.

In order for plants to really thrive, understanding their watering needs is crucial: while some species may appreciate a regular soaking, others (succulents, for instance) won't like being overwatered. Supplying the right nutrition to growing plants is key to good health and longevity, too.

Conserving water

Water is a precious resource. When you first start gardening, it's easy to head straight for the faucet to fill up your watering can, but the impact on the environment (and your water bill) can become hard to ignore. Instead, consider saving "gray" or used water. After a bath or washing the dishes, allow the water to cool and pour it into your watering can. As long as it's not too soapy or greasy, it will be fine for plants—although seedlings always need clean tap water as they are at a sensitive stage of growth.

For bigger gardens, consider buying a rain barrel—a big container that will collect and store rainwater, ready for use during drier spells. This can be connected to a downspout from a gutter (for instance, from a shed, greenhouse, or the house) to channel and store run-off water from the roof.

You can also slow down moisture loss from beds and borders using a mulch. This is a thick layer of material, such as sand, gravel, or bulky organic matter (bark chips, shredded bracken,

Watering young plants
After planting and transplanting, always water thoroughly and regularly even if the ground appears moist.

KEEP YOUR
landlord
IN THE LOOP

Ask your landlord about connecting a rain barrel to a downspout. This will allow you to harvest runoff from the roof, making it even easier to collect rainwater and keep the garden looking its absolute best.

or manure), that can be applied to moist soil. A mulch can also suppress weeds, while organic mulches help feed the soil, too (see opposite). While the soil is moist, apply a 2–4-in- (5–10-cm-) thick layer over the beds and around plants. Don't apply mulch to frozen ground, as this will seal in the cold.

Tips for good watering

- Water either in the evening or first thing in the morning. These are the coolest parts of the day, when water is less likely to evaporate and your plants' roots can absorb the water easily.
- Don't shower the whole plant, but direct water onto the soil, around the roots where it's most needed.
- For large plants, use a hose if you have one. No need to invest in a fancy sprinkler head—just direct water straight to the plants' roots.
- Prioritize watering young or newly planted plants, and those in containers (see opposite). Don't worry too much about established plants (more than three years old). They may wilt a little on hot days, but they should survive even a dry summer without extra assistance.

Watering lawns

The idea that a lawn needs to be green and pristine all summer is both impractical and environmentally problematic. There is nothing wrong with a well-established lawn turning slightly brown in a heatwave. This is natural, and the grass will recover once the rain returns. In dry spells, keeping grass at a slightly longer length helps it cope with drought.

Lawn length
A slightly longer lawn will withstand drought better than one mowed very short, but may still turn slightly brown in a dry spell.

Watering containers

Plants in containers need watering more often than those planted in the ground. Make sure to give them a good drink regularly, especially during hot spells, when the soil in their pots can quickly dry out. To help them retain water longer during heatwaves, stand potted plants in saucers or old plates—but remove them by fall, to stop the soil becoming saturated.

If you have a lot of new plants and little time to water them, consider investing in an automatic watering system. These are porous tubes laid around plants in borders, which release a steady drip of water run by a timer you can set to suit your garden's needs. For potted plants, drippers with thin pipes connected to a main pipe are most effective.

Feeding plants

Like humans, plants need both food and water. This is especially crucial if plants are in pots, where they have a restricted root run and cannot access nutrients in open soil. Incorporating slow-release fertilizer pellets or an organic feed when planting up containers is an easy way of boosting their nutritional content; alternatively, use a liquid feed once a fortnight during the summer.

Plants in beds and borders have better access to nutrients. However, they can struggle to yield the best results if grown in poor soil, so I suggest feeding the soil with mulches or pelleted manure. In established beds and borders, apply a layer of organic mulch to the soil when the ground is moist. There's no need to mix it in, as the worms will take it below the surface and help it decompose. Any organic mulch is beneficial: bark chips, manure, homemade compost (see pp.176–177), or well-rotted leaves (known as leaf mold) would all work well. Ideally, apply these products to established beds just before rain is forecast.

Watering and mulching
Water raised beds regularly (above left) so the water soaks into the soil. Applying a layer of organic mulch to damp soil (above right) helps the soil retain moisture.

Keeping plants in check

Managing plants in smaller gardens can be a bit of a challenge, especially if they outgrow their space or turn out to be more vigorous than expected. If you find your space losing definition and becoming overgrown, it's time to bring out the pruners or the hedge clippers.

There can be a fine line between allowing plants to develop a gentle softness in their shape, perhaps even mingling a little with one another, and letting them lose all definition and outgrow their space. If left unchecked, certain plants can end up dominating or even causing structural damage, so follow the pruning advice below to keep your space at its best.

Trees

Aside from removing dead, damaged, or diseased stems, the only pruning you should expect to do to a small tree is to remove the occasional lower branch if you need to make some space beneath it. Before you remove any branches, check the view behind to make sure that you won't reveal an eyesore during the pruning process.

As a rule of thumb, pruning should generally take place in winter, when the tree is dormant. Using a small, sharp folding saw, carefully cut through the branch next to the branch collar (the wrinkled bark that surrounds the point where the branch emerges from the trunk). Do not be tempted to cut it flush: while this might look and feel tidier, it removes the important callus material the tree uses to heal the pruning cut. Equally, avoid leaving too much of a stub sticking out, as this could lead to the tree developing a fungal infection.

For any bigger tree-pruning tasks— say, if a large branch needs to be removed, or the tree itself has grown too tall and may be causing structural issues—inform your landlord, as this may need to be dealt with by a professional.

Climbers

Depending on what climber you have, the pruning needs can differ quite significantly. As such, try to identify your climber and research its pruning needs before you begin. While an incorrect pruning technique will

seldom kill a climber, you may lose out on flowers or fruits if you trim it back too far or at the wrong time of year.

Try to keep climbers within their allotted space by tying or guiding them onto their designated wires, trellis, or fence, and keeping them from scrambling into nearby beds or up trees. Evergreen climbers such as ivy or star jasmine (*Trachelospermum*) can grow heavy and build up large volumes of growth if they are left unpruned year after year, and may eventually either fall off their support structure or even pull down a weak fence or trellis.

If you have inherited a space with an unruly climber, the solution may be to cut the plant back hard

Keeping a climber in its space
Removing any stems that are growing outward keeps the climber fairly flat to the wall. From time to time, a larger stem may need to be removed using a pruning saw.

KEEP YOUR *landlord* IN THE LOOP

It's worth discussing with your landlord how large or established shrubs and hedges have been pruned in the past. Tall hedges can be physically challenging to trim, and it is best to be aware of the landlord's expectations before things outgrow their space. It may be better for everyone to call in a professional if the work will be too laborious or time-consuming.

Pruning after flowering

Lavender needs to be cut back after it has flowered to keep its neat shape. Flower stems need to be removed with a small amount of leafy stem. Avoid cutting into old wood as it doesn't regrow easily.

needs can vary from shrub to shrub. If there is a mystery shrub in your yard that your landlord cannot identify, speak to any horticulturally-minded friends and family for advice, or use a plant identification app.

Many established summer-flowering shrubs need to have one-third of their old, woody stems cut back down to ground level each year after flowering; after pruning, they would also benefit from a layer of mulch (see p.165), particularly if they are growing in poor soil.

Some shrubs, such as viburnums and mock oranges (*Philadelphus*), if they are getting too large for the space, will bounce back from a hard or renovation prune (see opposite) with vigor. On the other hand, evergreens like rosemary or Californian lilac (*Ceanothus*) will not take favorably to hard or renovation pruning.

The type of pruning to avoid is simply cutting back a shrub to achieve a "tidy" shape. Done at the wrong time or to the wrong plant, this can mean that you end up losing some or all of the flowering stems, leaving a mass of unproductive, congested stems that just look awful. In the worst-case scenario, it can even kill the plant.

using hedge clippers. If you need to do this, time it for either before or after bird nesting season (which runs from late winter to midsummer), and check thoroughly before you begin cutting for any sign of nesting birds.

Shrubs

Established shrubs will often respond well to being pruned. As well as keeping them in good shape, pruning can encourage flowers and reduce the risk of the plant becoming congested with woody, unproductive stems. As with climbers, pruning

Hedges and clipped shrubs

Hedge plants, such as boxwood (*Buxus*) or yew (*Taxus*), are best clipped in mid- to late summer, after the first flush of growth. This timing is ideal because hedges seldom put on much more growth after this stage, meaning that they will stay neat through the winter. In addition, any birds that might have nested in the hedge should have raised their young and moved on by this time, meaning that it should be safe to prune. However, it isn't uncommon for some birds to nest late (or for a second time in the year) so do try to peer inside the hedge before you begin.

Depending on the size of the hedge, you can use either hand shears or an electric trimmer to cut back excess foliage. Trim the hedge back to your desired proportions, while aiming to keep the top of the hedge narrower and the base wider. If the top is left wider than the base, it can prevent sunlight reaching the lower parts of the hedge, resulting in a bare base. If the hedge has completely overgrown its allocated space, a renovation prune may be needed. This involves intentionally cutting back into old, unproductive wood to bring the hedge's width and height back into check. Beech (*Fagus*), hornbeam (*Carpinus*), and privet (*Ligustrum*) all respond quickly and readily to this process. Renovation pruning is best carried out in winter, when the plant is dormant, but do check with your landlord before starting. You should mark out the intended scale and shape of the hedge with bamboo canes and string, so you can make sure that you're working in a straight line.

Choosing the right tools
An electric trimmer achieves great results on large hedges (see left), while pruners may be enough to prune back climbers.

Keeping plants healthy

Plant health is similar to human health, in that prevention is better than cure. Aim to meet your plants' care needs to avoid problems, and learn to manage any pests that may be particularly troublesome.

Right plant, right place
As important as good watering and feeding, providing the correct light and temperature is key to good plant health.

Understanding plant health can often be a case of trial and error. By being patient and watching your garden grow—seeing what flourishes and what fails—you can learn from you mistakes and improve as a gardener.

Encouraging plants to thrive

The golden rule for plant health is to place plants in the conditions that best suit them. For example, a sun-loving succulent in deep shade will be as unhappy as a shade-loving fern in full sun. In the wrong situation, a plant will struggle to grow well, and if further stresses are added, such as irregular watering or lack of access to nutrients (see pp.162–165), pests and diseases move in.

If you find that a plant is struggling to grow, find out more about where it thrives naturally: if it is from a sheltered woodland environment with filtered light and you have it on a windy rooftop terrace, chances are it will never be happy. Fortunately, if many of your plants are in pots, you can move them around to more suitable locations. If your plant is in the best position and still is not looking good, review how you're watering and feeding it.

Dealing with common pests

Pests are a fact of life in the garden, but there are ways to reduce them. Ultimately, it is best to tolerate small levels of pest damage as pests are part of the wider ecosystem, and obliterating them from the garden can be harmful to other animals in the food chain (see pp.172–175). I'm very grateful to our resident blackbird for the snail patrol duties she performs in my yard, but I do wonder if she'd be there if I didn't provide the water feature she drinks from and the bird seed she dines on with the sparrows.

- **Slugs and snails** are often responsible for eating young leaves. During the day they go to cool, dark, damp spaces to hide, before appearing at night to eat your finest foliage, so check for

> **In the wrong situation, a plant will struggle to grow well, and if further stressed by lack of water or nutrition, pests and diseases can soon move in.**

hiding places in and around your plants and remove them by hand.
- **Sap-sucking insects,** such as aphids, feed on tender new shoot tips, weakening the plants' growth and distorting their leaves. Reduce their numbers by blasting them off with a water hose, and by encouraging natural predators such as birds, frogs, and ladybugs into your garden to feast on them.
- **Vine weevils** lay eggs in pots, and their larvae eat the roots of the plants within, sometimes causing death. Succulents, heucheras, and ivies are particularly susceptible. Apply nematodes (microscopic creatures that feed on vine weevils) in early fall to prevent damage.

Pest watch
Snails can often be found lurking in and around containers, while aphids will cluster on plants' soft, green new growth.

Supporting nature

In urban environments, gardens and outdoor spaces play a vital role in supporting local biodiversity. Even if you're only renting for a year or so, it's easy to make your space a wildlife-friendly place.

Plants for pollinators
Simple flowers attract the most pollinators. Highly bred flowers with lots of petals are often hard for insects to access.

There are so many ways you can work to make your rental space kinder to the planet and a welcoming place for all kinds of wildlife. Over the next few pages, I've suggested a few key steps you can take.

Some of the best solutions are the simplest: avoid using weedkiller and pesticides; choose alternatives to single-use plastics wherever available; and buy peat-free potting mix (or make your own—see pp.176–177) to avoid the environmental impact associated with using peat.

Planting for all wildlife

The best way to support local wildlife is to have as many different kinds of plants as you can. Plants that flower at different times of year (not just summer) provide fruit or berries for food, and often nectar for insects, early and late in the year when it is scarce. Evergreen plants that offer shelter over winter or nesting sites are also valuable.

Plants provide food and habitats for all insects, including pollinators like bees and butterflies, as well as pests (see pp.170–171). Slugs, snails,

Food and shelter
A shrub (above) may provide berries as well as shelter for birds, while allowing a path to grow a little messy (right) leaves opportunities for birds and insects to find food.

and aphids are a vital part of the food chain and their presence should be tolerated as much as possible. In my garden, snails live among the ivy on one of my walls and feed on the leaves. I don't mind this too much, because allowing the ivy to be nibbled is a lot more eco-friendly than laying down slug pellets to protect my ornamentals. That said, do keep an eye out to make sure slug and snail populations aren't out of control.

Keep things untidy

Tenants have a responsibility to keep their gardens neat—often, it's in the rental agreement. But tidiness can be a problem for wildlife, since many beetles and other insects—which are as important to ecosystems as birds and colorful butterflies—appreciate the shelter of a wilder corner. To encourage more wildlife, try to strike a balance without allowing the space to get out of control.

The first time I saw a hibernating hedgehog in my parents' yard was when we never got around to clearing fallen leaves from along the base of a wall. Instead they were hauled into a corner, where the hedgehog had created its winter refuge.

If you have a tree or large shrub, consider keeping pruning to a minimum. By tolerating a little disorderliness, you can provide places for birds and small mammals to shelter from predators, while also potentially allowing the tree or shrub to flower and produce berries.

Extra food and water

In my yard, the sparrows chatter from dawn to dusk as they visit my bird feeders, providing plenty of birdsong and entertainment. Offering food and water is probably the quickest way to encourage bird activity in the yard, particularly in winter. By stocking a simple bird feeder with seeds, peanuts, or suet, you can attract a variety of species, including chickadees, finches, and woodpeckers.

Position the feeder in a high spot, where predators are unlikely to reach, and clean it every few weeks to keep your avian visitors healthy. For water, a simple dish can provide much-needed drinking and bathing opportunities, especially in freezing weather—keep

Adding places for birds
Birdhouses and feeders can be colorful and add personality to your space. Our sparrow visitors don't seem to mind our eccentric feeding stations!

the water fresh and refill it often. If you have space for something a little more ornamental, consider creating a mini-pond or water feature (see pp.140–147).

Birdhouses

In urban spaces, birds can often have trouble finding places to nest, so if your landlord agrees to it, consider putting up a birdhouse. Different bird species use houses with different-size holes; start by feeding the birds to see what species appear and choose a house with those species in mind.

Choose a location on a wall or tree that is not too exposed to driving winds, rain, or full sunshine. Fix the birdhouse at least 6–10 ft (2–3 m) above ground with a clear flight path, and secure it in place with its supplied attachments. In the fall, clean out any old nests or debris when the birdhouse is empty. For more information, check the Audubon Society website.

Remember that birds may take many months to start using a house, so you may find that it's still occupied by the time your lease ends. Don't take it down; instead, let it be a parting gift to the local birdlife—and make sure the next tenants know about the house and how to clean it, too.

Insect refuges

While they may not be as immediately appealing as birds, insects and other invertebrates are just as important to welcome into our outdoor spaces. An "insect hotel" offers nooks and crannies for shelter, breeding, and

Insect hotel
This store-bought insect hotel has holes of different sizes for solitary bees to lay eggs as well as a vertical slot for butterflies.

hibernation away from predators and severe weather. An insect hotel can be bought, or just as easily made with sections of bamboo cane, pine cones, and terra-cotta pots stuffed with woody prunings. "Bee hotels" are similar, and are designed for solitary bee species like miner, mason, and leafcutter bees to lay their eggs. Position your bee hotel where it will get the morning sun, as the heat will energize the bees, which are quite docile and wonderful to observe.

If you have woody cuttings from pruning a tree or hedge, make a mini-log pile in a wild corner. These appeal to beetles, which in turn may become a source of food for birds and other visitors. Use the largest logs you can find (and are able to handle), and partially bury the bottom logs. Roughly chopped logs for wood-burning stoves can often be bought and used for log piles.

Composting

Every household generates organic waste, whether it's potato peelings, tea bags, and cardboard packaging from the kitchen, or weeds, grass, and hedge clippings from the yard. Composting offers an eco-friendly way of disposing of that waste, by turning it into nutritious compost to use in the garden.

Everybody who has the means to do so should compost their household and garden waste. It's not an option for every renter, but if you have some room in your yard to accommodate a compost pile and expect your tenancy to last for at least another year, read on.

Compost pile basics

To get started, you'll need a simple compost bin. Typically, this will be a container with a flap at the base for removing compost, and a lid at the top where you add fresh organic waste. Bins can be bought cheaply from garden centers, and may be made from wood or recycled plastic.

Compost bins tend not to have a base, to ensure that they have plenty of drainage. Stand the bin directly onto open ground, if any is available.

Composting garden waste
Add garden waste to your pile: grass clippings count as green waste, while thin, woody twigs count as brown.

If your outdoor space is paved over, you can still use a bin: just add a few shovelfuls of soil in the bottom before you start to fill it up, if you are able to.

Position the bin in a shady spot. Ideally, you want it to be out of sight—but not so far away that you won't want to venture out to it in winter with your kitchen waste!

Composting alternatives

If you don't have room for a full-size compost bin, there are smaller (often pricier) alternatives that are designed to reach higher temperatures more quickly, which speeds up the composting process. You could also look into wormeries or Bokashi bins, which also process waste on a smaller scale.

What to compost

To produce good compost, you need to follow a simple recipe. First, you need "brown waste": this is dry, organic material, such as cardboard or newspaper. You'll then need "green waste," which includes the likes of vegetable peelings, grass clippings, and other leafy garden waste.

Aim for a ratio of 80 percent green waste to 20 percent brown. If you have too much brown waste, nothing will happen; if you have too much green waste, you'll end up with a soupy mess. If you don't have enough green waste to add to meet the ratio, you can add accelerants to aid the process. These are coarse granules available to buy and are easy to apply to the mix.

Aim for 80 percent green waste to 20 percent brown. Add too much brown waste and nothing will happen, while too much green will result in a soupy mess.

Don't add cooked food waste, as this will attract rodents. Woody material, such as the stems of pruned shrubs or even large bunches of dead cut flowers, may take a long time to break down, so cut these up into small pieces to speed up the process.

What happens next

Expect the composting process to take anything from six months to a year. Bigger volumes of waste create more heat, which can speed up the process slightly. It helps the process if you can periodically turn or mix the contents of the compost bin with a fork, but this isn't essential.

If you're using a store-bought bin with a small flap at the base, don't be tempted to block it up to prevent rodents from getting in. The composting process needs air to circulate, or else the contents will stagnate and smell.

You might find that what seemed like masses of waste will only turn into a small amount of compost, but this gives you room to add more to your pile over time, producing more compost. This finished compost can be spread onto beds and borders as a mulch (see p165). No need to dig it in—just apply a generous layer and the worms will do the rest.

Weeding

No matter what kind of outdoor area you have, weeds are an inevitable part of gardening. To keep your space looking good (and your landlord happy), they are best dealt with sooner rather than later—but that doesn't mean you need to reach for the weedkiller.

Cutting back young weeds
On a sunny or windy day, use the blade of a garden hoe to sever the roots of young weed seedlings.

Weeds have a bad reputation, but you have to respect their resilience. Put simply, a weed is just a plant in the wrong place. By their very nature, they are successful plants: quick to grow, quick to flower, and therefore quick to spread their seeds around. Even if you somehow cleared your entire yard of weeds, before long a fresh batch of seeds would blow in on the wind and start again.

Due to their vigorous nature, weeds can overwhelm other plants growing in the same space as they compete for light, water, and nutrients. They can cause beds to look unsightly, and may also harbor slugs and snails, which will damage other plants.

Annual vs perennial weeds

Not all weeds are alike. As with many herbaceous plants, they can generally be divided into two main types: annuals and perennials. The likes of bitter cress, chickweed, and cleavers are all

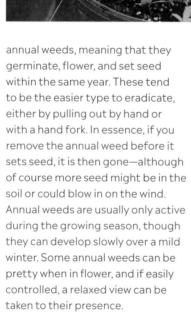

Weeds in pots
Check new plants when you buy them for any hitchhiking weeds such as this *Oxalis* growing among the crown of an ornamental grass.

with alarming vigor if they are particularly well-established. You can dig them up with a spade or rip them out with a garden fork, but it can be incredibly challenging to remove every part of the root system, and if just a small piece of the root remains, the weed can regrow within weeks to make its unwanted presence known.

Prevention is best

A few weeds may be unavoidable, but you can keep their numbers down. There are a few simple tricks you can use to keep them at bay:

- Avoid constantly disturbing the soil in beds and borders. Weed seeds germinate when light triggers their growth, so even if you have removed every weed from a border, if you then go on to "fluff up" the soil, you will end up bringing more seeds to the surface, encouraging them to sprout. The less you dig, the better.

- Apply a thick mulch around new plants. Not only will this help retain moisture (see pp.163–164), but it will effectively bury any annual weeds lurking on the surface of the soil, slowing down or preventing their growth.

- Inspect newly bought plants for weed seedlings. Not even nurseries and garden centers are completely immune from annual weed seeds finding their way into the soil.

annual weeds, meaning that they germinate, flower, and set seed within the same year. These tend to be the easier type to eradicate, either by pulling out by hand or with a hand fork. In essence, if you remove the annual weed before it sets seed, it is then gone—although of course more seed might be in the soil or could blow in on the wind. Annual weeds are usually only active during the growing season, though they can develop slowly over a mild winter. Some annual weeds can be pretty when in flower, and if easily controlled, a relaxed view can be taken to their presence.

Perennial weeds, like greater bindweed, horsetail, and couch grass, are trickier. As the name suggests, this kind of weed can live for years, developing extensive root systems as time goes by. Their roots may also become entangled with those of ornamental plants. They might die back over winter, but come spring they reemerge—sometimes

Dealing with weeds

In established beds, borders, and even between paving and in gravel areas, weed seedlings can start to appear as soon as spring arrives. If the space has been neglected by previous tenants, there may well be several years' worth of weed seeds lurking in the soil, just waiting to germinate. To win the battle, you'll need to clear as many weeds as you can before they set seed. As the old gardener's saying warns us, one year's seeding is seven years' weeding!

No matter how many weeds your yard has, unless you're faced with a serious problem (see opposite), a "little and often" approach is the best way to deal with them. With a hand fork and a bucket, work your way around and clear as much as you can. A hoe can also be used to quickly deal with large amounts of small annual weeds; use the blade to slice along at soil level, severing young stems from their roots. If you can, use the hoe on a sunny or windy day, as this weather will quickly cause the weeds to perish.

After a few sessions, you should hopefully find that you have fewer and fewer annual weeds to deal with. It's always easier to remove young seedlings than well-established plants, so try to weed at least a little every week if you can.

Persistence is key with perennial weeds. Try to dig out as much of the root as possible, going as deep as you are able, and should it return in the summer, weaken it by pulling the tops off, or wiping it with weedkiller gel. If an area is riddled with perennial weeds, a weed-suppressant fabric laid over the top of the soil, then covered with mulch, can also help block out light and prevent growth.

Using weedkiller

As a last resort, you may need to use weedkiller. Many are now made from natural rather than synthetic ingredients, but even these should be used with caution, following the manufacturer's instructions. Weedkiller will damage whichever plant they land on, so if using a spray, wait for a still day to prevent the wind blowing particles onto other plants. Gels and wipe-on treatments offer a more targeted application.

Removing annual weeds
A hand fork is ideal for digging out small annual weeds, roots and all.

Weeds to watch out for

Some weeds are so persistent, the efforts and sometimes budgets required to clear them would likely need to fall onto a landlord's shoulders. It may be better for tenants to try and manage them at a low level, with some acceptance that they will exist in the space.

Japanese knotweed

This invasive weed is a serious environmental concern as it is so difficult to eradicate. If you spot it, alert your landlord and ask them to consult local authorities about dealing with it.

Greater bindweed

This climbing weed is deep-rooted and rapidly smothers other plants with its heart-shaped leaves and milky white, trumpetlike flowers. To remove, try forking out the roots or severing it with a hoe at ground level.

Horsetail

Established populations of horsetail are almost impossible to eradicate. Grow taller plants around it to hide it, although it's not too unattractive itself.

Couch grass

This fast-spreading weed invades any available space via underground stems, poking up through paving, gravel, and other plants. Fork out the white roots with a border fork.

Maintaining hard surfaces

Fences, paving, decking, and other hard surfaces can appear tired and unappealing if they aren't given a little care and attention now and then. Take some time to care for them and you will improve the appearance of the whole space.

Hard surfaces can often be overlooked in rental spaces. Sagging fences, algae-slick decking, and sparsely graveled areas can all be dealt with.

Paving and decking

If you have a damp, shady yard, chances are you'll know how decking or paving can double up as an ice rink in cold or wet weather. Algae can grow on top of a layer of moisture, quickly becoming a hazard. You can remove this with organic algae cleaner, which is specially designed for patios and decking; follow the manufacturer's instructions for how to apply it.

Alternatively, rent or borrow a pressure washer: this will enable you to effectively clear away heavy algal buildup, and remove other dirt and

Fresh gravel
Topping up gravel from time to time makes the area look well cared for and neat.

Routine care
Keeping your paving slabs free of algae (right) gives them a crisper look and makes them safer. A regular application of paint (far right) helps your fence look good and last longer.

grime in the process, too. Pressure washing is a slow but satisfying job: systematically working from A to B, blasting away all dirt and debris, often giving surfaces a new lease on life afterward. Take care with the joints between paving as pressure washing can blast out the cement or sand which then leaves fresh space for weeds. Don't fret too much about removing moss or lichen from paving. They rarely cause problems, and in my opinion tend to make a space more attractive and natural-looking.

Gravel

Over time, gravel areas can start to deplete and look patchy. Mix in a fresh bag of gravel and the area will immediately look tidier, and the added stones will help keep the area free of weeds (see p.163).

Fences and wood surfaces

Wood needs to be treated from time to time, to keep it looking fresh and to prevent rot and decay. A wide range of paints, oils, and preservatives are available for this purpose. Apply during dry weather, and brush the fence down beforehand to remove loose debris and plant growth.

Clearing away debris

Allowing fall leaves and other plant debris to build up can lead to decay over time. Use a stiff broom to keep the space well-swept, and make sure that strip drains and drain pipes are clear to allow water to flow freely.

KEEP YOUR *landlord* IN THE LOOP

Discuss any costs associated with the upkeep of hard surfaces, such as renting a pressure washer or buying wood-treatment products—after all, these are permanent features in their property.

Working with the seasons

It's best to work with the seasons so you are prepared for when tasks need doing, and to give plants the best conditions for success. This isn't always easy as a renter, but is possible with a bit of thought.

Fall color
A busy time in the garden, fall is the season to prepare for the following year. Vivid foliage and late flowers are the highlights.

Fall

This is one of the busiest times in the garden. The ground is typically moist from early fall rain but not yet cold from winter frosts, making it an ideal time to plant, lift, and divide a wide range of plants. This season is also a great time to plan how you want your outdoor space to look the following year. A lot of work invested toward the end of fall is paid back the following spring. Look out for bargains at end-of-season plant sales, too.

If you're moving into a new place in fall, one of the best things you can do is plant bulbs, such as daffodils or crocuses, into pots or in beds. That way, as you start to assess your space and plan what you want to do with it, you know that you're guaranteed a burst of color the following spring.

What to plant now
- Spring-flowering bulbs (see pp.96–103).
- Perennials such as *Geum* and red hot poker (see pp.128–129).

- Trees (see p.133, pp.136–137).
- Lay turf (see pp.150–152).

Taking care of your garden
- Protect tender plants that cannot cope with the winter cold by bringing them indoors.
- Divide mature or congested perennials, replanting the divisions if wished (see p.123).
- Sow grass seed in bald lawn patches (see p.152).
- Treat potted plants with nematodes to protect against vine weevil attack (see p.171).
- Clean out birdhouses ahead of the nesting season (see p.175).
- Compost or dispose of spent annuals and other bedding plants.
- Collect fallen leaves and put them into a compost pile, or into bags to make leaf mold (see pp.176–177).

Winter

During the winter, the outdoor world can appear to be asleep. While there isn't much to do in the garden now, there are still a few tasks you can tackle—although it's best to avoid gardening when the ground is frozen. If the weather is particularly bad, use it as an opportunity to research and buy seeds for next year.

If you're moving into a new place in winter, spend some time cutting back stems of perennials that have died back and dealing with overgrown plants. You could also clear and clean existing surfaces if they need it. If you have open ground, wait to see what comes up in spring.

What to plant now
- Winter-flowering bedding plants (see pp.46–49).

Taking care of your garden
- Cut back the dead stems of herbaceous plants (see p.121) or deciduous grasses.
- Shake heavy snow off evergreen trees so they do not break under the weight.
- Clean out ponds, removing excess algae or fallen leaves.
- Top-up gravel paths.
- Prune dead, damaged, or diseased stems on trees when it is not freezing (see p.166).
- Prune overgrown hedges to stimulate spring growth (see p.169).
- Feed the birds and ensure they have a water supply (see pp.174–175).
- Remove weeds (see pp.178–181).
- Apply mulch to borders when the ground is not frozen (see p.179).
- Clean areas of paving or decking (see pp.182–183).

Winter peace
There are few urgent winter tasks, so it's a good time to plan ahead and to enjoy the bare bones of the garden outside.

Spring

This is perhaps the most fun time of the gardening year, as you prepare for the growing season ahead. I love to sit outside after a spring rain shower to soak up the sounds and smells of spring growth.

Keep an eye on the weather forecast; while it can be a beautiful time of year, it can also be very cruel if late frosts strike. Make sure tender plants are brought in or protected if the temperature looks set to dip below freezing. Toward the end of spring, harden off plants grown under cover so you can plant them out when the risk of frost has passed (see p.54).

If you move into your new home in spring, you can get started with planting up containers with bedding plants or even vegetables. Look at neighboring yards to see what grows well to give you planting ideas, or check out pp.114–117 to find some inspiration.

Springing into life
Leaves, shoots, and flowers start to emerge and it's a busy time for sowing and planting—but also for protecting tender plants and new growth.

What to plant now

- Seeds of annual plants (see pp.52–55) and some vegetables (see pp.114–117).
- Summer pot displays of tender plants and summer bedding plants (see pp.46–49 and pp.80–83).
- Tender vegetables and herbs.
- Summer-flowering bulbs such as lilies and gladioli (see p.97).

Taking care of your garden

- Insert supports for perennials whose stems might topple or flop over (see p.121).
- Give overgrown shrubs a hard (or "regenerative") prune—but check they are free of nesting birds first!
- Begin watering container plants as temperatures rise, or set up an irrigation system (see p.165).
- Paint fences before plants grow up too tall in front of them (see p.183).
- Keep on top of weeds, which start growing quickly (see pp.178–181).

Summer

Now is the time to make the most of your garden: sit outdoors with a cup of coffee, a glass of wine, or friends. I am not so good at stopping to enjoy my little rented garden, but every gardener deserves to spend time among their plants.

Many relaxing summer hours are taken up with watering, especially plants in containers. Even if you do get summer showers, it will likely not be enough to keep potted plants fully hydrated, so check on them regularly to make sure they don't dry out.

Summer relaxation
While there are still watering and maintenance tasks to do, this is the time to relax and enjoy your garden.

If you move in during the summer, and there are already some plants, try to identify them while they are in flower and leaf to help with planning for next year.

What to plant now
- Foliage plants in containers, with a few bedding plants (see pp.62–63).
- Sow quick-growing vegetable crops (see pp.114–117).

Taking care of your garden
- Water plants well, especially as temperatures rise (see p.165).
- Remove and compost or dispose of dead flower heads.
- Harvest herbs, fruits, and vegetables.
- Place houseplants outdoors in a shady space.
- Mow lawns as desired (see p.151).
- Continue to watch out for weeds.

Index

Acknowledgments

Author acknowledgments

I'm beyond grateful to the teams at the RHS and DK for encouraging me to write my first book under their prestigious brands, namely Chris Young and Sue Biggs from the RHS and Ruth O'Rourke, Amy Slack, and Lucy Philpott from DK who have been with me every step of the journey. The gardening world is such a helpful and generous place, and I'm grateful to Armando Raish of Treebox and the team at the Gedney Bulb company for their donations and the ever-helpful Alex Swyer from the Wisley Plant Centre.

A huge thank you must go to friends who let us barge into their gardens for photos and to build projects, namely Amy and Lucy in Putney, Lorna in Chelsea, Giulia and Luca in Fulham, Peter and Freddie Bear in Wisley and Ash and Ben in Wembley. The wonderful photos in the book are courtesy of the superstar who is the fabulous Sarah Cuttle, under the watchful eye of the lovely Nigel Wright.

Finally, a shout-out to my parents who supported and encouraged my love of plants from as long as I can remember, a seed which was undoubtedly sowed by my grandma, and to my partner Kishan for always being by my side and listening to me moan of my terrible neck ache as I wrote this whole book bent over a tiny laptop at the kitchen table!

Publisher acknowledgments

DK would like to thank Giulia and Luca Griotti, Peter Jones, Lorna Vaughan, and Ashley San Pedro for kindly allowing us to photograph their outdoor spaces. We would also like to thank Sarah Smithies and Nic Dean for picture research, Lucy Philpott and Conor Kilgallon for editorial assistance, John Tullock for consulting, Francesco Piscitelli for proofreading, and Vanessa Bird for indexing.

Picture credits

The publisher would like to thank the following for their kind permission to reproduce their photographs:

(Key: a-above; b-below/bottom; c-centre; f-far; l-left; r-right; t-top)

4 GAP Photos: Richard Bloom - Katharina Nikl Landscapes. **6 Image Professionals GmbH:** living4media / Jalag / Petra Stange. **14 GAP Photos:** Clive Nichols - Designer: Charlotte Rowe, London. **16 GAP Photos:** Matteo Carassale - Design: Stefano Baccari. **18 GAP Photos:** Lynn Keddie. **20 Getty Images:** E+ / Anchiy. **21 GAP Photos:** Annie Green-Armytage (b); Matteo Carassale - Garden design: Gaia Chaillet Giusti del Giardino. (t). **22 Clive Nichols. 26 GAP Photos:** Anna Omiotek-Tott - Designed by Sarah Keyser. CouCou Design (tr); Friedrich Strauss (tl). **28 GAP Photos:** Paul Debois. **30 GAP Photos:** Paul Debois

(br). **The Garden Collection:** FP / Ute Klaphake (bl). **31 GAP Photos:** Jerry Pavia (tl); Friedrich Strauss (tr). **32 Clive Nichols. 35 GAP Photos:** Nicola Stocken (tl, tr). **36 Alamy Stock Photo:** Made and Found (bc). **38 The Garden Collection:** FP / Liz Eddison. **40 GAP Photos:** Heather Edwards - Design: Jill Foxley. **42 GAP Photos:** Jonathan Buckley - Design: Sarah Raven. **43 GAP Photos:** Jacqui Hurst. **44 GAP Photos:** (b); Friedrich Strauss (t). **45 GAP Photos. 50 Dorling Kindersley:** Mark Winwood / Ball Colegrave. **51 Dreamstime. com:** Thomas Brandt (c); Pimmimemom (t); Jacqueline Van Kerkhof (cl); Sandis Vāgners (cb); Tom Meaker (bl); Norman Chan (bc). **53 GAP Photos:** Christa Brand - Weihenstephan Gardens. **54 GAP Photos:** Gary Smith. **55 GAP Photos:** (br); Jonathan Buckley - Demonstrated by Carol Klein (bl). **57 Alamy Stock Photo:** David Bleeker (tl); Diliana Nikolova (bl). **Dorling Kindersley:** Mark Winwood / Ball Colegrave (c). **60 Alamy Stock Photo:** Steffie Shields (bl). **GAP Photos:** Brent Wilson (t). **61 Press Loft:** Dobbies. **62 Dorling Kindersley:** Mark Winwood / RHS Wisley (bc). **63 Dorling Kindersley:** Mark Winwood / RHS Wisley (cr). **GAP Photos:** Bjorn Hansson (bl); Dave Zubraski (tl). **65 Alamy Stock Photo:** Andreas von Einsiedel. **66 GAP Photos:** Paul Debois - Designer: James Walsh (tr); Colin Poole (tl). **67 GAP Photos:** Mark Bolton. **69 Alamy Stock Photo:** blickwinkel. **72 Dreamstime.com:** Alla Sravani. **73 Alamy Stock Photo:** blickwinkel (tl). **Dreamstime.com:** Feathercollector (c); Simona Pavan (cl). **Thompson & Morgan:** (clb, bl, bc). **74 The Garden Collection:** FP / Liz Eddison. **76 Clive Nichols. 78 GAP Photos:** Mark Bolton (t); Doreen Wynja (b). **79 GAP Photos:** Elke Borkowski. **82 GAP Photos:** Friedrich Strauss (bl). **84 Alamy Stock Photo:** RM Floral (c). **Dreamstime.com:** Thomas Brandt (bl); Whiskybottle (bc). **85 Dorling Kindersley:** Mark Winwood / Capel Manor College, Designer - Irma Ansell, 'The Mediterranean Garden' (tl). **Dreamstime.com:** Blackregis (c). **86 Clive Nichols. 87 Clive Nichols. 88 The Garden Collection:** FP / Liz Eddison. **89 GAP Photos:** Paul Debois (br); J S Sira - Design: Mike Harvey. **94 Dorling Kindersley:** Mark Winwood / RHS Wisley. **95 Alamy Stock Photo:** David Robertson (clb). **Dorling Kindersley:** Mark Winwood / RHS Chelsea Flower Show 2014 (cl); Ian Redding (c); Mark Winwood / RHS Wisley (bc). **Dreamstime.com:** Akintevsam (cb). **96 Clive Nichols. 97 GAP Photos. 98 GAP Photos:** Nicola Stocken (tr); Friedrich Strauss (tl). **99 The Garden Collection:** FP / Sibylle Pietrek. **103 GAP Photos:** (cr). **104 123RF. com:** lianem. **105 Alamy Stock Photo:** thrillerfillerspiller (bl). **Dorling Kindersley:** Mark Winwood / RHS Wisley (tl, c); Mark Winwood / Marle Place Gardens and Gallery, Brenchley, Kent (cl). **Dreamstime.com:** Seawhisper (bc). **GAP Photos:** Lynn Keddie (clb). **107 Clive Nichols. 108 The Garden Collection:** FP / Helga Noack (br). **Clive Nichols:** (tl). **109 Image Professionals GmbH:** living4media / Medri – Szczepania. **115 Dreamstime. com:** Ellen Mol (cl); Volatan1 (tl). **116 Dreamstime.com:** Nikolay Dimitrov (bl); Stockcreations (t). **117 Thompson & Morgan:** (br). **118 GAP Photos:** Rob Whitworth. **120 GAP Photos:** Anna Omiotek-Tott. **122 GAP Photos:** Nicola Stocken. **123 GAP Photos:** Friedrich Strauss (b); Rob Whitworth (t). **128**

Dreamstime.com: John Caley (bc). Getty Images / iStock: Kat Robertson (c). Thompson & Morgan: (bl). 129 Dreamstime.com: Angelacottingham (c); Michal Paulus (tl, cl). Getty Images / iStock: Alastair James (bc); Liudmyla Liudmyla (cr). 130 GAP Photos: Anna Omiotek-Tott - Design: Tom Massey. 132 GAP Photos: Jacqui Hurst (tl); Joanna Kossak - Designer: Andrew Wilson and Gavin McWilliam - Sponsor: Darwin Property Investment Management (tr). 136 GAP Photos: Michael Howes (bl). 138 Dreamstime.com: Irene Majano Maganto (c). GAP Photos: Mark Bolton (bl). 139 Dorling Kindersley: Mark Winwood / RHS Wisley (cl, bc). Dreamstime.com: Sarah Marchant (cr). GAP Photos: Tim Gainey (c). Getty Images / iStock: Whiteway (tl). 141 GAP Photos: Nicola Stocken. 142 GAP Photos: Leigh Clapp. The Garden Collection: FP / Liz Eddison (br). 148 Alamy Stock Photo: Martin Fowler. 149 Alamy Stock Photo: Florapix (tl). Dreamstime.com: Stefan Rotter (bl); Maren Winter (c). Getty Images / iStock: nickkurzenko (cl). 150 GAP Photos: Nicola Stocken. 153 The Garden Collection: FP / Liz Eddison (br). Image Professionals GmbH: living4media / Celeste Najt (tl). 155 GAP Photos: Clive Nichols - Designer: Ana Sanchez-Martin of Germinate Design. 159 Dorling Kindersley: Dreamstime.com: Sandra Standbridge (bc). Dreamstime.com: Arinav (cb); Digitalimagined (c); Denis Doronin (clb).. GAP Photos: Nova Photo Graphik (tl). 160 GAP Photos: Matteo Carassale - Project by Marilu' Biffis. 162 GAP Photos: FhF Greenmedia.164 The Garden Collection: FP / Jürgen Becker (bl). 168 GAP Photos: Thomas Alamy. 169 GAP Photos: Richard Bloom (br); Bjorn Hansson (bl). 170 GAP Photos: Annaick Guitteny / Designer: Amelia Bouquet - Sponsors: London Stone, Practicality Brown, Urbis Design. 171 GAP Photos: Jonathan Buckley (bl); Howard Rice (bc). 172 GAP Photos: Nicola Stocken. 173 Dreamstime.com: 1000words (tr). GAP Photos: Zara Napier (tl). 175 Dreamstime.com: Matthias Lindner. 176 GAP Photos: Maxine Adcock. 178 GAP Photos: Tim Gainey. 179 Dreamstime.com: Matthew Howard. 180 GAP Photos. 182 GAP Photos: Lynn Keddie. 183 GAP Photos: (tl); Richard Bloom (tr). 184 GAP Photos: Nicola Stocken. 185 GAP Photos: Janet Johnson. 186 GAP Photos: Friedrich Strauss. 187 Clive Nichols.

All other images © Dorling Kindersley

About the author

When **Matthew Pottage** was appointed Curator of RHS Wisley, the Royal Horticultural Society's flagship garden, he became the youngest Curator in the Society's history. Since then, he has managed the garden through significant changes, including the creation of RHS Hilltop ("the Home of Gardening Science") and its associated gardens, as well as a new arrival experience for the garden, an Exotic Garden, and the Wisteria Walk.

Matthew can often be heard on the RHS's *The Garden* podcast, as well as on BBC Radio 2 and Radio 4, most notably as a panelist on *Gardeners' Question Time*. He writes frequently for a range of gardening literature, and sits on the advisory committee for the Chelsea Physic Garden in London.

Dubbed by *The Times* as "*the* gardener for Generation Rent," Matthew lives in west London with his partner Kishan. Matthew's passion for houseplants, trees, conifers, succulents, and variegated plants has transformed their rented flat into an oasis of greenery.

Penguin Random House

DK LONDON
Project Editor Amy Slack
Project Designers Louise Brigenshaw, Harriet Yeomans
Editor Jane Simmonds
Designer Amy Child
US Editor Megan Douglass
Senior Production Editor Tony Phipps
Production Controller Rebecca Parton
Jacket Designer Amy Cox
Jacket Coordinators Lucy Philpott, Jasmin Lennie
Managing Editor Ruth O'Rourke
Managing Art Editors Marianne Markham, Christine Keilty
Consultant Gardening Publisher Chris Young
Art Director Maxine Pedliham
Publishing Director Katie Cowan

ROYAL HORTICULTURAL SOCIETY
Consultant Simon Maughan
Publisher Rae Spencer-Jones

First American Edition, 2022
Published in the United States by DK Publishing
1450 Broadway, Suite 801, New York, NY 10018

A catalog record for this book
is available from the Library of Congress.
ISBN 978-0-7440-2692-4

DK books are available at special discounts when purchased in bulk for sales promotions, premiums, fund-raising, or educational use. For details, contact: DK Publishing Special Markets, 1450 Broadway, Suite 801, New York, NY 10018
SpecialSales@dk.com

Printed and bound in China

For the curious
www.dk.com

MIX
Paper from responsible sources
FSC
www.fsc.org
FSC™ C018179

This book was made with Forest Stewardship Council ™ certified paper— one small step in DK's commitment to a sustainable future. For more information go to www.dk.com/our-green-pledge.